Your exclusive ticket to

a Gooseberry Patch adventure!

When a new season is drawing near, there's nothing more exciting than pulling out favorite recipes and getting inspired. As an **exclusive, free gift** for Gooseberry Patch email subscribers, Vickie and JoAnn are creating **limited edition collections** of the very best of the seasons.

These handcrafted seasonal guides (**$9.95 value**) are full of our favorite recipes, inspiring photos, DIY tips and holiday ideas – you'll be celebrating all season long! A new issue will be released 4 times per year and each one is available for a limited time only.

D1469211

If you haven't signed up yet, come aboard. Your subscription is your ticket to year 'round inspiration – and it's completely free!

www.gooseberrypatch.com/signup

Visit our website today, add your name to our email list, and you'll be able to download our latest seasonal preview instantly!

Find Gooseberry Patch
wherever you are!

www.gooseberrypatch.com

Call us toll-free at 1·800·854·6673

YOUR recipe could appear in our next cookbook!

Share your tried & true family favorites with us instantly at

www.gooseberrypatch.com

If you'd rather jot 'em down by hand, just mail this form to...

Gooseberry Patch • Cookbooks – Call for Recipes
2545 Farmers Dr., #380 • Columbus, OH 43235

If your recipe is selected for a book, you'll receive a FREE copy!

Please share only your original recipes or those that you have made your own over the years.

Recipe Name:

Number of Servings:

Any fond memories about this recipe? Special touches you like to add
or handy shortcuts?

Ingredients (include specific measurements):

Instructions (continue on back if needed):

Special Code: **cookbookspage**

Over ➚

Extra space for recipe if needed:

Tell us about yourself...

Your complete contact information is needed so that we can send you your FREE cookbook, if your recipe is published. Phone numbers and email addresses are kept private and will only be used if we have questions about your recipe.

Name:

Address:

City: State: Zip:

Email:

Daytime Phone:

Thank you! Vickie & Jo Ann

Good-For-You

Everyday Meals

Gooseberry Patch
2545 Farmers Dr., #380
Columbus, OH 43235

www.gooseberrypatch.com

1•800•854•6673

Copyright 2014, Gooseberry Patch 978-1-62093-087-8
First Printing, January, 2014

U.S. to Metric Recipe Equivalents

Volume Measurements

1/4 teaspoon	1 mL
1/2 teaspoon	2 mL
1 teaspoon	5 mL
1 tablespoon = 3 teaspoons	15 mL
2 tablespoons = 1 fluid ounce	30 mL
1/4 cup	60 mL
1/3 cup	75 mL
1/2 cup = 4 fluid ounces	125 mL
1 cup = 8 fluid ounces	250 mL
2 cups = 1 pint =16 fluid ounces	500 mL
4 cups = 1 quart	1 L

Weights

1 ounce	30 g
4 ounces	120 g
8 ounces	225 g
16 ounces = 1 pound	450 g

Oven Temperatures

300° F	150° C
325° F	160° C
350° F	180° C
375° F	190° C
400° F	200° C
450° F	230° C

Baking Pan Sizes

Square		Loaf	
8x8x2 inches	2 L = 20x20x5 cm	9x5x3 inches	2 L = 23x13x7 cm
9x9x2 inches	2.5 L = 23x23x5 cm	Round	
Rectangular		8x1-1/2 inches	1.2 L = 20x4 cm
13x9x2 inches	3.5 L = 33x23x5 cm	9x1-1/2 inches	1.5 L = 23x4 cm

Contents

Dedication

To moms & dads everywhere
who believe a home-cooked
meal is better than fast food
any day of the week.

Appreciation

To all of you who shared
your tastiest family-pleasing
recipes...thanks!

Off to a

Fresh Start

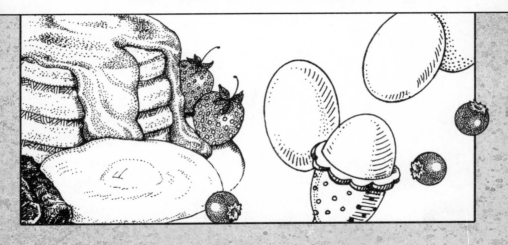

Blueberry Cornmeal Pancakes

Eleanor Dionne
Beverly, MA

*Since we like cornmeal muffins as well as anything with blueberries,
it's no surprise that these pancakes became a family favorite.*

1 c. all-purpose flour
1 c. cornmeal
2 T. baking powder
1 T. sugar
1/2 t. salt

1-1/2 c. orange juice
3 T. canola oil
1 egg, beaten
1 c. blueberries, thawed if frozen

In a bowl, mix together flour, cornmeal, baking powder, sugar and
salt. Add juice, oil and egg; stir well. Gently fold in blueberries. Heat a
lightly greased griddle over medium-high heat. Pour batter onto griddle
by 1/4 cupfuls. Cook pancakes until bubbles appear around the edges;
flip pancakes and cook on other side. Makes about 8 pancakes.

The number-one tip for speedy meals! Before you start cooking,
read the recipe all the way through and make sure
you have everything you'll need.

Funny texture

Off to a Fresh Start

Fruity Cinnamon Oatmeal

Jill Ball
Highland, UT

There's nothing more perfect than sitting by the fireplace watching the snow fall while eating a warm bowl of oatmeal. This recipe is one of our favorites...it's warm, filling and yummy.

3 c. milk or water
4-inch cinnamon stick
1-1/2 c. long-cooking oats, uncooked
1 apple, peeled, cored, and diced
1/4 c. plus 1 T. maple syrup, divided

1 t. cinnamon
1/2 t. allspice
Garnish: pomegranate seeds, cinnamon

Combine milk or water and cinnamon stick in a small saucepan. Bring to a boil over high heat. Stir in oats and apple; reduce heat to medium. Cook for 5 to 10 minutes, stirring often, to desired consistency. Remove from heat; discard cinnamon stick. Stir in 1/4 cup syrup and spices. Ladle into bowls; top each with a drizzle of remaining syrup, some pomegranate seeds and a sprinkle of cinnamon. Makes 4 servings.

Try steel-cut oats in any recipe that calls for regular long-cooking oats. Steel-cut oats are less processed for a pleasing chewy texture you're sure to enjoy.

Baked Eggs in Tomatoes

Jill Burton
Gooseberry Patch

*So pretty for a brunch...a delicious way to enjoy
heirloom tomatoes from the farmers' market.*

6 tomatoes, tops cut off
   and reserved
salt and pepper to taste
1/2 c. corn, thawed if frozen
1/2 c. red pepper, diced
1/2 c. mushrooms, diced

2 T. cream cheese, softened
   and divided
6 eggs
2 t. fresh chives, minced
1/4 c. grated Parmesan cheese

With a spoon, carefully scoop out each tomato, creating shells.
Sprinkle salt and pepper inside tomatoes. Divide corn, red pepper and
mushrooms among tomatoes; top each with one teaspoon cream
cheese. In a bowl, whisk together eggs, chives and additional salt and
pepper. Divide egg mixture among tomatoes; top with Parmesan
cheese. Place tomatoes in a lightly greased 9"x9" baking pan; replace
tops on tomatoes. Bake, uncovered, at 350 degrees until egg mixture
is set, about 45 to 50 minutes. Serve warm. Makes 6 servings.

When making Baked Eggs in Tomatoes, set the tomatoes
in a muffin tin...they'll stay upright in the oven.
A handy tip for your favorite stuffed peppers too.

Off to a Fresh Start

Mom's Best Orange Muffins

Kelly Patrick
Ashburn, VA

This recipe takes me back to my younger days when I'd give Mom a call and ask her to whip up a batch just for me. She used to make them years ago when I was training to run a marathon. Oranges and plump raisins add a tasty kick...yum!

1-1/2 c. golden raisins
2 c. boiling water
1-1/2 c. oat bran
1 c. wheat bran
1 c. all-purpose flour
1 c. ground flax seed
1 T. baking powder
1/2 t. salt

2 oranges, peeled, quartered
   and seeds removed
1 c. brown sugar, packed
1 c. buttermilk
1/2 c. canola oil
2 eggs
1 t. baking soda

Place raisins in a bowl; cover with boiling water and set aside. Meanwhile, in a separate bowl, mix together oat and wheat bran, flour, flax seed, baking powder and salt; set aside. In a blender, combine remaining ingredients except raisins; process well. Add orange mixture to bran mixture; stir just to moisten. Drain raisins well and pat dry; fold into batter. Spoon batter into 24 paper-lined or greased muffin cups, filling 2/3 full. Bake at 375 degrees for 18 to 20 minutes, until a toothpick inserted in the center tests clean. Makes 2 dozen.

Garden Bounty Egg Bake

Lisa Sanders
Shoals, IN

I came up with this easy recipe to help my husband Jim enjoy eating more vegetables. He loves eggs, so what better way to get him to eat veggies! Yummy served with biscuits and jelly. For an extra-hearty breakfast, add one cup cooked and crumbled bacon or sausage.

1 doz. eggs
1/2 c. milk
1 T. dried parsley
1 t. dried thyme
1 t. garlic powder
salt and pepper to taste
1 T. olive oil
8-oz. pkg. sliced mushrooms
1/2 c. onion, diced

1/2 c. green pepper, diced
1/2 c. carrot, peeled and
   shredded
1/2 c. broccoli, chopped
1/2 c. tomato, chopped
1 c. shredded mild Cheddar
   cheese
Optional: hot pepper sauce

In a bowl, whisk together eggs and milk; stir in seasonings and set aside. Heat oil in a large ovenproof skillet over medium-high heat. Add all vegetables except tomato; sauté until crisp-tender. Add tomato to skillet. Pour egg mixture over vegetable mixture; remove skillet to the oven. Bake at 350 degrees for about 15 to 20 minutes, until a knife tip inserted in the center tests clean. Sprinkle with cheese; return to oven until cheese melts. Serve with hot pepper sauce, if desired. Makes 6 servings.

Hard-boiled eggs are terrific to have on hand for speedy breakfasts, easy sandwiches or even a quick nutritious snack. Use eggs that have been refrigerated at least seven to ten days...the shells will slip right off.

Off to a Fresh Start

Raspberry Cream Smoothies

Shirl Parsons
Cape Carteret, NC

*I have been making these refreshing smoothies for years.
They're a delicious, nutritious way to start your day.*

3 c. frozen raspberries
1 c. banana, cubed and frozen
2 c. orange juice
2 c. frozen vanilla yogurt

2 c. fat-free reduced-sugar
   raspberry yogurt
2 t. vanilla extract

In a blender, combine frozen fruit and remaining ingredients. Process until smooth; stir, if needed. Pour into chilled glasses. Makes 8 servings.

Healthy Strawberry Drink

Renae Scheiderer
Beallsville, OH

This is a beverage my husband Al loves! Especially on hot summer days when juicy strawberries are in season.

2 c. fresh or frozen strawberries,
   hulled
2 c. fat-free milk

2/3 c. calorie-free powdered
   sweetener
5 to 7 ice cubes

Combine all ingredients in a blender; process until smooth. Pour into chilled glasses. Makes 4 servings.

Try this simple fruit smoothie...
just substitute milk for water with a
favorite frozen fruit juice concentrate.
Pour into the blender and blend
until frothy. So refreshing!

Cinnamon-Almond Granola

Amy Bradsher
Roxboro, NC

*My family loves to make breakfast parfaits with this granola.
We each layer our favorite fruit and creamy yogurt with granola
to make a healthy, colorful breakfast in a hurry!*

5-1/2 c. long-cooking oats,
   uncooked
1/2 c. sliced almonds
1/2 c. roasted sunflower kernels
1/2 c. sweetened flaked coconut

1/2 c. honey
1/2 c. butter, melted
1 t. cinnamon
1 t. almond extract

In a large bowl, mix together oats, almonds, sunflower kernels and
coconut. In a separate bowl, stir together remaining ingredients. Pour
honey mixture over oat mixture; stir until well mixed. Divide mixture
between 2 lightly greased 15"x10" jelly-roll pans, spreading as
evenly and thinly as possible. Bake, uncovered, at 200 degrees for
20 minutes; stir well and return to oven. Repeat steps 2 times, until
lightly toasted and golden. Let cool completely; store in an airtight
container for up to 2 weeks. Makes 16 servings.

Toss together ripe summer fruits like blueberries, strawberries
and kiwi for a tempting fruit salad. Drizzle with a dressing made
by whisking together 1/2 cup honey, 1/4 cup lime juice and
one teaspoon lime zest...yummy!

Off to a Fresh Start

Hearty Breakfast Quinoa

Jill Ball
Highland, UT

I'm always looking for hearty, healthy, yummy breakfast ideas. This one is great! My family likes it, and I feel good that they're starting the day right.

1 c. non-fat skim milk
1 c. water
1/4 t. salt
1 c. quinoa, uncooked
1 t. cinnamon

2 c. blueberries or raspberries, thawed if frozen
1/3 c. chopped toasted walnuts
3 t. sweetened flaked coconut
1 T. sugar

In a saucepan over medium heat, stir together milk, water, salt and quinoa. Bring to a boil. Reduce heat to medium-low; cover and cook for 15 minutes, or until quinoa is tender and liquid is absorbed. Remove from heat; let stand, covered, for about 5 minutes. Gently stir in cinnamon and berries. Just before serving, top with walnuts and coconut; sprinkle with sugar. Makes 4 servings.

Try using regular or low-fat milk, soy milk, almond milk or coconut milk in breakfast dishes...there's sure to be one that suits your family!

Laurel's Nutty Granola

Laurel Liebrecht
Yakima, WA

*My family loves this granola! I've tried many recipes, but this is
by far our favorite. Add a dollop of yogurt...wonderful!*

1/4 c. butter, melted
1/4 c. honey
3 c. long-cooking oats,
   uncooked
1 c. sweetened flaked coconut

1 c. roasted sunflower kernels
1 c. chopped or slivered almonds
1 c. chopped pecans
1-1/2 t. cinnamon
2/3 c. raisins

In a lightly greased 13"x9" baking pan, stir together butter and honey.
Add remaining ingredients except raisins; mix well. Bake, uncovered,
at 350 degrees for about 15 minutes, stirring several times. Continue
baking for 10 minutes, or until mixture is lightly golden. Remove from
oven; cool slightly and stir in raisins. Let cool completely; store in an
airtight container for up to 2 weeks. Makes 8 servings.

Invite friends over for a farmstyle breakfast served on
the porch. Make it picture-perfect with a yard or two of
striped cotton ticking on the table and a milk bottle filled
with just-picked posies...it's super simple.

Off to a Fresh Start

Go-Go Juice

Carolee Jones
Homer, AK

*My kids often don't have much time for breakfast, but I know if
I hand them a bottle of Go-Go Juice, they'll be off to a good start!
You'll find protein powder and spirulina powder in the health food
section of the supermarket.*

16-oz. can frozen orange juice
    concentrate
10 c. cold water

1/4 c. vanilla-flavored protein
    powder
1 to 2 t. spirulina powder

Combine frozen orange juice and remaining ingredients in a large
pitcher. Whisk or stir until frothy. Keep refrigerated. Makes
12 servings.

Honey comes in lots of flavor varieties. Seek out a local
beekeeper at the farmers' market and try a few samples...
you may find a new favorite!

Breakfast Salad with Poached Eggs

Kelly Serdynski Gray
Weston, WV

This dish may sound odd, but it is really delicious...quick to make too. I serve it often for brunch, while my son requests it often for dinner. I like to add two poached eggs per salad, but you may prefer just one.

8 slices bacon, halved
8 c. spring lettuce mix
2 c. shredded Cheddar cheese
1 c. sliced mushrooms

1 c. sliced black olives
4 roma tomatoes, quartered
Garnish: ranch salad dressing

Cook bacon in a skillet over medium heat until crisp; drain. Meanwhile, prepare Poached Eggs in a separate skillet. Divide lettuce among 4 plates. With a slotted spoon, place 2 eggs atop lettuce on each plate; sprinkle with cheese while still hot. Arrange vegetables around eggs; arrange bacon on top. Drizzle with salad dressing; serve immediately. Makes 4 servings.

Poached Eggs:

2 c. water
2 t. white vinegar

8 eggs, divided

In a skillet over medium-high heat, bring water and vinegar to a simmer. Crack 2 eggs into water. Cook for 5 to 7 minutes, to desired doneness. Remove eggs with a slotted spoon; repeat with remaining eggs.

Add more flavor to your cup of coffee! Just wet the paper filter before brewing.

Off to a Fresh Start

Judy's Famous Banana Muffins

Judy Mitchell
Huntley, IL

Our local newspaper featured me as "Cook of the Week" with this recipe! I found the original recipe many years ago and have revised it over the years. It's a favorite of family & friends.

3 very ripe bananas, mashed
2 eggs, beaten
1/2 c. canola oil
1/2 c. plus 1 T. sugar, divided
1/2 c. quick-cooking oats,
    uncooked
1/2 c. whole-wheat flour

1/2 c. all-purpose flour
1/2 c. wheat germ
1 t. vanilla extract
1 t. baking powder
1/2 t. baking soda
1/4 t. salt
1/2 c. chopped walnuts

In a large bowl, stir together bananas, eggs, oil and 1/2 cup sugar until combined. Add remaining ingredients except walnuts and remaining sugar; stir just until blended. Spoon batter into 12 paper-lined muffin cups, filling about 2/3 full. Sprinkle tops with walnuts and remaining sugar. Bake at 350 degrees for 20 to 25 minutes, until golden and a toothpick tests clean. Let muffins cool in tin for 5 minutes; remove to a wire rack and cool completely. Makes one dozen.

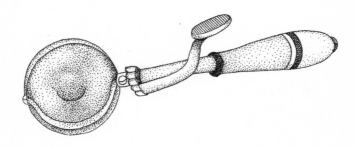

Use an old-fashioned ice cream scoop to fill muffin cups with batter...no drips, no spills and muffins turn out perfectly sized.

Savory Zucchini Frittata
Jacqueline Young-De Roover
San Francisco, CA

This fast and tasty recipe uses up a lot of zucchini! Sometimes I will use a blend of Parmesan, Romano and Gouda cheeses. Serve with a crisp vinaigrette-dressed salad for a lovely brunch.

2 T. olive oil
3 shallots, finely minced
4 cloves garlic, finely minced
6 zucchini, sliced 1/4-inch thick
   on the diagonal
1 doz. eggs, lightly beaten

salt and white pepper to taste
1 c. fresh Italian flat-leaf
   parsley, snipped
1 c. finely shredded Parmesan
   cheese

Add oil to a large skillet over medium heat; swirl to coat bottom and sides of pan. Add shallots and garlic; cook and stir for about one minute. Add zucchini; cook, stirring often, for 5 to 7 minutes, until crisp-tender. Remove pan from heat; add remaining ingredients and mix lightly. Spray a 9" round glass baking pan with butter-flavored non-stick vegetable spray. Spoon mixture into pan. Bake, uncovered, at 325 degrees until set, about 30 minutes. Serve warm or cooled. Makes 6 servings.

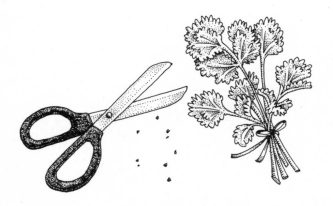

Keep a pair of kitchen scissors handy...they make quick work of snipping fresh herbs and chopping green onions.

Off to a Fresh Start

Homestyle Country Sausage

Linda Murray
Brentwood, NH

Comfort food doesn't have to be unhealthy. I make this sausage every year for our Christmas breakfast. It took awhile for everyone to figure out that it was made with turkey! I often make one batch of this hot sausage as round patties, and another batch of oval patties omitting the cayenne pepper...it's easy to tell the difference.

1 tart apple, peeled, cored and
   shredded
1/2 c. cooked brown rice
2 T. onion, grated
2 cloves garlic, minced
1-1/2 t. dried sage

1/2 t. dried thyme
1/8 t. allspice
1 t. salt
1/2 t. pepper
Optional: 1/8 t. cayenne pepper
1 lb. lean ground turkey

In a large bowl, combine apple, rice, onion, garlic and seasonings. Crumble turkey into apple mixture; mix well with a large spoon. Form into 8 patties, 1/2-inch thick. Cover a broiler pan with aluminum foil and spray with non-stick vegetable spray. Place patties on pan. Broil for 4 to 6 minutes on each side, or until juices run clear. Makes 8 servings.

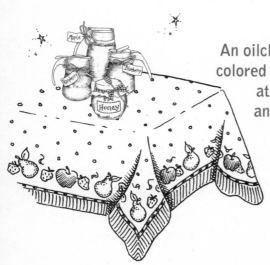

An oilcloth tablecloth with brightly colored fruit and flowers is cheerful at breakfast...and sticky syrup and jam spills are easily wiped off with a damp sponge.

Asparagus & Mushroom Omelet

Audrey Lett
Newark, DE

A delicious way to savor the first tender asparagus of springtime.
Add a sprinkle of shredded cheese, if you like.

1/2 lb. asparagus, trimmed and
    cut into 1-inch pieces
2 T. butter, divided
1/2 lb. sliced mushrooms
1 clove garlic, minced

4 eggs, lightly beaten
2 T. milk
3/4 t. dried basil
1/2 t. salt
1/8 t. pepper

In a saucepan over medium heat, cover asparagus with water.
Bring to a boil and cook until crisp-tender, about 4 minutes; drain.
In a skillet over medium heat, melt one tablespoon butter. Sauté
mushrooms and garlic in butter until tender and moisture has
evaporated, 5 to 7 minutes. Add mushroom mixture to asparagus;
keep warm. In a bowl, whisk together eggs, milk and seasonings. Melt
remaining butter in skillet; swirl to coat bottom and sides. Add egg
mixture. As eggs cook, gently lift up edges with a spatula and let
uncooked egg run underneath until set. Spoon asparagus mixture
onto one half of omelet. Slide omelet onto a plate; fold over. Cut into
wedges. Makes 4 servings.

Mushrooms are flavorful, filling and low in calories. Add them
to egg dishes, pasta sauces, soups and wherever else you'd like
a punch of flavor. Store mushrooms, unwashed, in a
paper bag in the fridge.

Off to a Fresh Start

Red Pepper & Roasted Garlic Quiche

Jennifer Niemi
Meadowvale, Nova Scotia

This quiche is easy enough to make for an everyday brunch or lunch, yet special enough to serve to company. Roasted garlic is delicious and simple to make, but does take a little time...roast several bulbs at once, then freeze the pulp for future recipes!

1/4 c. butter
1-1/2 c. onion, finely chopped
1 c. milk, divided
3-1/4 t. all-purpose flour
1 t. dried thyme
3 eggs
1/2 t. sugar

1/8 t. salt
1/8 t. pepper
1/2 c. red pepper, finely chopped
1 c. shredded sharp white
 Cheddar cheese
9-inch pie crust

Prepare Roasted Garlic; set aside. Melt butter in a heavy skillet over medium heat. Add onion; cook until translucent, about 5 minutes. Add Roasted Garlic pulp, 1/2 cup milk, flour and thyme to skillet. Cook and stir until thickened, 3 to 5 minutes. Remove from heat. In a bowl, beat together eggs, remaining milk, sugar, salt and pepper. Stir in red pepper, cheese and onion mixture; pour into unbaked pie crust. Bake at 425 degrees for 15 minutes. Reduce heat to 350 degrees. Bake an additional 25 to 30 minutes, until a knife tip inserted in center tests clean. Cut into wedges. Makes 6 servings.

Roasted Garlic:

1 whole garlic bulb

1 t. olive oil

Remove as much of papery peel from garlic bulb as possible; cut off top. Drizzle olive oil over bulb. Wrap in aluminum foil, sealing well. Bake at 275 degrees for one hour. Loosen foil, exposing garlic; bake an additional 25 to 30 minutes. Cool; press out pulp.

Banana Bread Pancakes

Amy Bradsher
Roxboro, NC

The first time I made these unusual-looking pancakes, my Little Man didn't want to try them, but he was hooked at the first nibble. My Big Helper, on the other hand, took one bite and yelled, "Mommy! These are delicious! I'll give you a hundred hugs and a hundred kisses for these!"

2 c. white whole-wheat flour
2 t. baking powder
1/4 t. salt
1 t. cinnamon
3/4 c. milk
1/4 c. honey

2 T. butter, melted
1 t. vanilla extract
3 ripe bananas, mashed
Garnish: maple syrup
Optional: chopped walnuts

In a large bowl, mix together flour, baking powder, salt and cinnamon. In a separate bowl, stir together milk, honey, butter and vanilla. Slowly pour milk mixture into flour mixture; stir well. Add bananas; stir to combine. Spoon batter by 1/3 cupfuls onto a lightly greased griddle over medium heat. Cook for 2 to 3 minutes, until bubbles begin to form on top; turn. Cook on other side for another 2 to 3 minutes, until golden. Serve topped with maple syrup and garnished with walnuts, if desired. Makes about one dozen pancakes.

Leftover pancakes are easy to store and reheat. Just freeze pancakes in plastic freezer zipping bags. To reheat, place pancakes in a single layer on baking sheets. Bake at 350 degrees for 5 to 10 minutes, then they're ready to be topped.

Off to a Fresh Start

Mom's Fruit Smoothies

April Haury
Paramus, NJ

*My kids love these smoothies. Sometimes I use two bananas if
I have some on hand that need to be used up. If you'd like
a thicker smoothie, add a little more frozen fruit. Enjoy!*

1-1/2 c. frozen peaches or
   strawberries
1 ripe banana, sliced

8-oz. container non-fat vanilla
   yogurt

Combine frozen fruit, banana and yogurt in a blender. Process until
smooth; pour into tall glasses. Makes 3 servings.

Energy Boost Smoothies

Evelyn Thorpe
Lodi, CA

*I'm not a coffee drinker, so this smoothie gives me the
boost of energy that I need first thing in the morning!*

1 ripe banana, sliced
3 to 5 strawberries, hulled
1/3 c. fresh or frozen blueberries
1 carrot, sliced
1 apple, cored and quartered

1 orange, peeled and sectioned
1/2 c. baby spinach
1 c. ice cubes
1/2 c. water
Optional: flax seed to taste

Combine all ingredients in a food processor or blender. Process until
smooth and well mixed; pour into tall glasses. Makes 2 servings.

Baked Breakfast Goodness

Kristy Markners
Fort Mill, SC

My two-year-old daughter just loves oatmeal. I got tired of fixing her the same old instant packet everyday, so I came up with this recipe. I like it just as much as she does! For a slimmed-down version, use unsweetened almond milk and powdered sweetener.

1/4 c. unsweetened applesauce
1/2 c. sugar or low-calorie
   powdered sweetener blend
   for baking
3 T. egg white substitute, beaten
1/2 c. milk or unsweetened
   almond milk

1-1/2 c. multi-grain hot cereal,
   uncooked
1 t. baking powder
1/2 t. cinnamon
1/8 t. ground ginger
1 banana, diced
1 /4 c. dried wild blueberries

Stir together applesauce, sugar, egg white and milk in a bowl. Add cereal, baking powder and spices; stir until well combined. Fold in fruit. Spoon into an 8"x6" baking pan sprayed with non-stick vegetable spray. Bake, uncovered, at 350 degrees for 30 minutes. Makes 4 servings.

Keep both early risers and sleepyheads happy with fresh, hot breakfasts...it's simple. Fill individual ramekins or custard cups with a favorite baked oatmeal or breakfast casserole and pop into the oven as needed.

Off to a Fresh Start

Overnight Apple-Cinnamon Oats
Dana Rowan
Spokane, WA

I was looking for a healthy, filling breakfast that I wouldn't have to fuss with early in the morning. This slow-cooker recipe is always a hit with the family. It's so nice to wake up to a warm breakfast!

2 apples, peeled, cored and
   chopped
2 c. milk
1-1/2 c. water
1/2 c. unsweetened applesauce
1 c. steel-cut oats, uncooked

1/4 c. brown sugar, packed
1 T. butter, diced
1 t. cinnamon
1/4 t. salt
Garnish: maple syrup, milk,
   applesauce, chopped walnuts

Spray a slow cooker with non-stick vegetable spray. Add all ingredients except garnish; stir. Cover and cook on low setting for about 7 hours. If desired, stir in a little more milk or water to thin to desired consistency. Spoon into bowls; garnish as desired. Makes 6 servings.

Fill a muffin tin with yummy oatmeal toppings...brown sugar, raisins, chopped nuts and even chocolate chips. So easy for everyone to help themselves!

Black Bean Breakfast Burritos

Meg Dickinson
Champaign, IL

My husband and I love the idea of eating breakfast for dinner, but plain old pancakes and eggs were getting boring. I tried this combination, and it was a huge hit. No more ho-hum breakfast foods!

2 T. olive oil
1/2 c. onion, chopped
1/2 c. green pepper, chopped
3 cloves garlic, minced
16-oz. can black beans, drained and rinsed
10-oz. diced tomatoes with green chiles

2 t. fajita seasoning mix
6 eggs
1/2 c. green onion, chopped
1 T. Fiesta Dip Mix
6 10-inch flour tortillas, warmed
1/2 c. shredded Cheddar cheese

Heat oil in a Dutch oven over medium heat. Add onion, green pepper and garlic; sauté until tender. Stir in beans, tomatoes and fajita seasoning. Bring to a simmer and let cook about 10 minutes. Meanwhile, in a bowl, whisk together eggs, green onion and one tablespoon Fiesta Dip Mix. Scramble egg mixture in a lightly greased skillet. To serve, top each tortilla with a spoonful of bean mixture, a spoonful of scrambled eggs and a sprinkle of cheese; roll up tortilla. Makes 6 burritos.

Fiesta Dip Mix:

2 T. dried parsley
4 t. dried, minced onion
4 t. chili powder

1 T. dried cumin
1 T. dried chives
1 T. salt

Mix all ingredients well; store in a small jar. Makes about 1/2 cup.

A super-easy fresh breakfast side dish...fruit kabobs!
Just slide strawberries, melon cubes, pineapple chunks,
grapes and orange wedges onto wooden skewers.

Off to a Fresh Start

Simple Southwest Omelet

Maxine Griffin
Heber Springs, AR

This yummy omelet goes together in a jiffy. Try Mexican-blend cheese for extra zest!

4 slices bacon, diced
1 jalapeño pepper, seeded and
   diced

4 eggs, beaten
salt and pepper to taste
1 c. shredded Cheddar cheese

In a skillet over medium heat, cook bacon until nearly crisp and golden. Add jalapeño pepper and cook until tender. Drain, reserving a small amount of drippings in skillet. Reduce heat to low; pour eggs over bacon mixture. Cook until almost set, gently lifting up edges with a spatula to let uncooked egg run underneath. When set, sprinkle with cheese; fold omelet in half and cut into wedges. Makes 4 servings.

When frying bacon for breakfast, reserve a few slices. Later, slice a homegrown tomato into thick slices and add crisp lettuce and country-style bread for a fresh BLT sandwich...lunch is served!

Orange Yogurt Pancakes

Larissa Miller
Bradley Beach, NJ

These pancakes are easy to make, fluffy and delicious. My cousin shared a version of this recipe with me, and I've modified it a bit. Have some fun...add chopped fruit or nuts to the batter too.

1-1/2 c. whole-wheat flour
1 T. brown sugar, packed
3/4 t. baking powder
1-1/2 t. baking soda
1/4 t. salt

2 eggs
1-1/2 c. non-fat vanilla yogurt
1/2 c. milk
1/2 c. orange juice
zest of 1 orange

In a large bowl, combine flour, brown sugar, baking powder, baking soda and salt; set aside. In a separate bowl, whisk eggs; stir in remaining ingredients. Add egg mixture to flour mixture. Stir until combined; let stand for several minutes. Pour batter by 1/4 cupfuls onto an oiled griddle over medium-high heat. Cook until small bubbles form around the edges; flip and cook until other side is golden. Makes about 8 pancakes.

Serve up a little whimsy with breakfast! Pour pancake batter into squirt bottles and squeeze the batter directly onto a hot, greased griddle to form bunnies, cats or your child's favorite animal.

Off to a Fresh Start

Colorful Fruit Soup

Irene Whatling
West Des Moines, IA

*This soup is so refreshing! My daughter requests it every summer.
Freshly ground black pepper complements sweet fruit wonderfully.*

1 c. seedless grapes, halved
1 c. blueberries
1/2 c. strawberries, hulled
   and diced
1/2 c. pineapple, peeled
   and diced

1/2 c. kiwi, peeled and diced
1 c. reduced-calorie apple juice
1/2 c. orange juice
1/4 t. pepper

Combine fruit in a large bowl. In a measuring cup, mix juices and
pepper; pour over fruit mixture. Stir gently. Cover and refrigerate until
serving time. Makes 6 servings.

A nutritious breakfast in a hurry! Toast half a whole-grain
bagel, then top with reduced-fat cream cheese and
sliced fresh strawberries.

Farm-Fresh Omelet

LaDeana Cooper
Batavia, OH

As our garden started producing lots of veggies, my kids started making up their own recipes. For once, Mom was the assistant! Here is an all-time favorite that they came up with. We like our vegetables crisp, but if you prefer them more tender, sauté before adding to the omelet.

2 eggs
1 T. milk
salt and pepper to taste
1 t. butter
1/2 to 1 t. green onion, thinly
    sliced

1 to 2 T. favorite vegetables like
    zucchini, yellow squash,
    asparagus or carrot, cut into
    thin sticks
Optional: diced tomatoes
2 T. shredded Cheddar cheese

Beat together eggs, milk, salt and pepper in a bowl; set aside. Melt butter in a skillet over medium heat; add egg mixture. Cook until set underneath; flip gently and cook other side. Top half of omelet with vegetables as desired. Sprinkle with cheese; fold over and turn out onto a plate. Makes one serving.

Omelets and frittatas are perfect for using up all kinds of
odds & ends from the fridge. Mushrooms, tomatoes and
asparagus are especially good with eggs. Slice or dice
veggies and sauté until tender...scrumptious!

Off to a Fresh Start

Scrambled Eggs & Sweet Onion

Amy Butcher
Columbus, GA

*My family enjoys these eggs in late spring, when the
sweet onions are harvested here in Georgia.*

1 T. olive oil
1 sweet onion, chopped
8-oz. pkg. sliced mushrooms
8 eggs, beaten

2 T. half-and-half
1 t. dried thyme
1/2 t. salt
1/4 t. pepper

Heat olive oil in a skillet over medium heat; add onion and
mushrooms. Sauté for 5 to 10 minutes, until onion is tender and
lightly golden; drain. In a bowl, whisk together remaining ingredients.
Pour egg mixture over onion mixture in skillet. Reduce heat to low and
cook, stirring occasionally, until eggs are set. Makes 6 servings.

Place onions in the freezer for just five minutes, then chop
with an extra-sharp knife...no more tears!

31

Peanutty Breakfast Wrap

Crystal Shook
Catawba, NC

In a hurry every morning? Don't leave home without breakfast!

8-inch whole-wheat tortilla
1 T. creamy peanut butter
1 T. vanilla yogurt
1 T. honey

1/4 c. granola
1/4 c. blueberries or
    strawberries, or 1/2 banana,
    diced

Spread one side of tortilla with peanut butter and yogurt. Drizzle with honey; sprinkle with granola and fruit. Roll up tightly. Serve immediately, or wrap tightly in plastic wrap and refrigerate. Makes one serving.

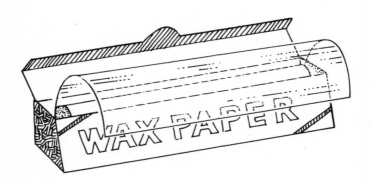

Take 'em along! Roll up a Peanutty Breakfast Wrap in
wax paper or plastic wrap, and it's ready for
an early morning picnic or mid-morning snack.

Off to a Fresh Start

Amazing Chocolate-Banana Smoothies

Marla Kinnersley
Highlands Ranch, CO

I've been making this recipe several mornings a week for years. My kids have no idea how good for them it is. They think I'm just a fun mom and that we're having dessert for breakfast!

2 ripe bananas, sliced and
    frozen
3-1/2 c. chocolate almond milk

2 t. creamy peanut butter
2 t. ground flax seed meal

Add frozen bananas and remaining ingredients to a blender. Process until smooth. Pour into tall glasses and serve. Makes 4 servings.

For a nutty taste and extra fiber, sprinkle wheat germ or flax seed onto bowls of yogurt or oatmeal and into muffin and pancake batter.

33

Oatmeal Waffles

Lisa McClelland
Columbus, OH

These waffles were a favorite holiday breakfast of mine when I was growing up. My mother didn't trust waffle mixes, so this is her from-scratch recipe. They are wholesome and yummy, especially when topped with warm cinnamon-apple compote.

1-1/2 c. all-purpose flour
1 c. quick-cooking rolled oats, uncooked
1 T. baking powder
1/4 t. sea salt
2 t. pumpkin pie spice
1 t. vanilla extract

2 eggs, lightly beaten
1-1/2 c. milk
6 T. butter, melted and slightly cooled
2 T. brown sugar, packed
Garnish: butter, warmed maple syrup

In a large bowl, mix together flour, oats, baking powder, salt, spice and vanilla; set aside. In a separate bowl, stir together remaining ingredients except garnish. Add egg mixture to flour mixture; stir until blended. Pour batter by 1/3 cupfuls onto a preheated, lightly greased waffle iron. Bake according to manufacturer's instructions. Serve topped with butter and maple syrup. Makes about 6 waffles.

Do you prefer to use egg whites instead of whole eggs in pancake and waffle batter? For each egg, substitute two egg whites or 1/4 cup egg substitute.

Off to a Fresh Start

Baked Blueberry Oatmeal

Sharon Newell
Hancock, MI

This is one of my favorite brunch recipes. It's easy and can be mixed up the night before. Even people who say they don't like oatmeal have been known to have seconds and even ask for the recipe! Try it with raspberries or blackberries also.

4 c. old-fashioned oats,
    uncooked
1 c. sugar
2 t. baking powder
2 c. milk
3/4 c. butter, melted and slightly
    cooled

4 eggs, beaten
3/4 c. applesauce
1 c. blueberries, thawed if frozen
Optional: brown sugar

In a large bowl, mix together all ingredients except blueberries and brown sugar. Spoon into a lightly greased 13"x9" baking pan. Add blueberries; push down into mixture. If desired, sprinkle brown sugar on top. Bake, uncovered, at 350 degrees for 40 minutes, or until golden on top. Makes 8 servings.

Enjoy fresh blueberries year 'round...freeze them during
berry season, when they are plentiful and inexpensive.
Spread ripe berries in a single layer on a baking sheet and
freeze until solid, then transfer to plastic freezer bags.
Later, pour out just the amount you need.

Broccoli Quiche Peppers

Cheri Maxwell
Gulf Breeze, FL

We love these colorful peppers for a brunch dish that's
just a little different. Sprinkle with mozzarella cheese, if desired,
after you take the peppers from the oven.

4 red, yellow or green peppers,
   tops cut off and reserved
1 c. broccoli, finely chopped
4 eggs

1/2 c. milk
1/2 t. garlic powder
1/4 t. Italian seasoning

Finely dice reserved tops of peppers; set aside. Place pepper shells upright in custard cups; set cups in a 9"x9" baking pan. Spoon 1/4 cup broccoli into each pepper; set aside. In a bowl, whisk together eggs, milk, diced pepper and seasonings; pour evenly into peppers. Bake, uncovered, at 325 degrees for 40 to 50 minutes, until peppers are tender and egg mixture is set. Let stand 5 minutes before serving. Makes 4 servings.

Add the nutty taste of whole grains to breakfast...they're delicious
and healthy too! Try toasted whole-wheat bread, multi-grain
English muffins and pancakes with a sprinkle of wheat germ
stirred into the batter.

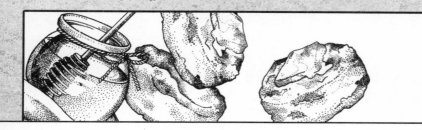

Hearty Soups &

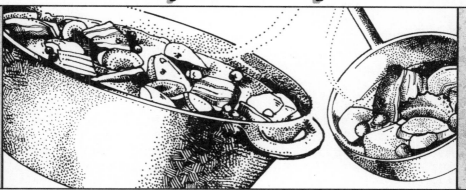

Fresh-Baked Breads

Vegetable Goodness Minestrone

Stefanie Schmidt
Las Vegas, NV

I love making this soup on cold nights! It has so much flavor...
every spoonful is healthy and comforting.

1-1/4 c. whole-wheat elbow
   macaroni or small shell
   pasta, uncooked
16-oz. pkg. frozen mixed
   vegetables
2 c. low-sodium vegetable broth
14-1/2 oz. can diced tomatoes

15-1/2 oz. can kidney beans,
   drained and rinsed
2 T. fresh parsley, chopped,
   or 2 t. dried parsley
1 t. Italian seasoning
1/4 t. pepper

Cook macaroni or pasta according to package instructions; drain.
Meanwhile, in a separate large saucepan over medium heat, cook
frozen vegetables in broth for 15 minutes, or until tender. Do not drain.
Add tomatoes with juice and remaining ingredients; stir in cooked
macaroni or pasta. Reduce heat to low; heat through. Makes
4 servings.

Don't hesitate to stock up on frozen
vegetables. Flash-frozen soon after
being harvested, they're available in
many varieties. Frozen vegetables
actually retain more nutrients than
fresh produce that has traveled
for several days before arriving
in the grocery's produce aisle.

Hearty Soups & Fresh-Baked Breads

Spaghetti Soup

Margie Bush
Peoria, IL

*I love to make homemade soups in the winter for my family.
Of all the soups I make, this is their favorite.*

1 lb. lean ground beef
1 onion, chopped
2 stalks celery, diced
1 green pepper, diced
2 carrots, peeled and diced
2 cloves garlic, minced
5 to 6 c. water
15-oz. can spaghetti sauce

2 14-1/2 oz. cans diced
   tomatoes
1/2 t. Italian seasoning
1/2 t. salt
1/4 t. pepper
1/2 c. spaghetti, uncooked and
   broken into 2-inch pieces

In a large skillet over medium heat, cook beef with onion, celery, green pepper, carrots and garlic until beef is browned and vegetables are tender. Drain; add water, sauce, tomatoes with juice and seasonings. Increase heat to medium-high. Bring to a boil; stir in spaghetti. Cook for 10 to 15 minutes, stirring frequently, until spaghetti is tender. Makes 10 servings.

Warm garlic bread makes any meal a little better! Cut a loaf of Italian bread in half lengthwise. Blend 1/2 cup softened butter with 2 minced garlic cloves, one tablespoon chopped fresh parsley and 1/4 cup grated Parmesan cheese. Spread over cut sides of bread and broil 2 to 3 minutes, until golden and bubbly. Slice and serve...mmm!

Tomato-Tarragon Soup

Rebecca Wood
Escondido, CA

Every year my vegetable garden overflows with vine-ripened tomatoes, and I'm always trying different ways to cook, can and serve them. This soup is one of my favorite dishes.

2 lbs. tomatoes
3 T. butter, divided
1 shallot, minced
2 cloves garlic, minced

2 T. all-purpose flour
salt and pepper to taste
2 T. fresh tarragon, chopped
1 T. fresh parsley, chopped

Peel tomatoes, reserving all the juice; strain seeds from juice. Chop tomatoes and combine with juice; set aside. Melt one tablespoon butter in a large saucepan over medium-low heat. Add shallot; sauté until translucent. Add garlic; sauté for one minute, just until golden. Melt remaining butter with shallot mixture. Stir in flour, salt and pepper; cook and stir until thickened and lightly golden. Stir in tomatoes and juice; add herbs. Increase heat to medium. Bring to a simmer; stir constantly until mixture begins to thicken. Reduce heat to low. Cover and simmer for 15 minutes. Cool slightly; purée soup in a blender until smooth. Return soup to saucepan. Warm through and serve hot, or cover, refrigerate and serve chilled. Makes 4 servings.

Need to add a little zing to a soup or stew? Just add a dash of herb-flavored vinegar...a super use for that bottle you brought home from the farmers' market.

Hearty Soups & Fresh-Baked Breads

Cheddar-Dill Corn Muffins

Vickie

These dressed-up corn muffins are scrumptious and simple to make.

1 c. cornmeal
1 c. all-purpose flour
1/3 c. sugar
2-1/2 t. baking powder
1/2 t. baking soda
1/4 t. salt
1 egg

3/4 c. milk
1-1/2 c. shredded sharp
    Cheddar cheese
1 c. corn, thawed if frozen
1/4 c. butter, melted
3 T. fresh dill, minced,
    or 1 T. dill weed

In a large bowl, mix cornmeal, flour, sugar, baking powder, baking soda and salt; set aside. In a separate bowl, whisk together egg and milk; stir in remaining ingredients. Add egg mixture to cornmeal mixture; stir just until moistened. Spoon batter into 12 greased or paper-lined muffin cups, filling 2/3 full. Bake at 400 degrees for about 20 minutes, until golden and a toothpick inserted in the center tests clean. Cool muffins in tin on a wire rack for 10 minutes before turning out of tin. Serve warm or at room temperature. Makes one dozen.

A big square of red-checked homespun fabric makes a cozy liner for a basket of warm muffins or rolls. You don't even need to hem the edges...just pull away the threads to create a fringe.

Chicken, White Bean & Pasta Soup

Lydia Edgy
Patterson, MO

This is such a healthy, satisfying soup. I always feel good when I serve it to my family.

1 onion, chopped
4 carrots, peeled and sliced
4 stalks celery, sliced
2 T. olive oil
4 c. low-sodium chicken broth
3 c. water, divided
2 to 3 boneless, skinless chicken
   breasts, cooked and diced

2 15-1/2 oz. cans Great
   Northern beans, drained
6 cherry tomatoes, diced
1/2 t. dried thyme
1/2 t. dried rosemary
salt and pepper to taste
1 c. rotini pasta, uncooked
1/2 lb. baby spinach

In a large saucepan over medium heat, sauté onion, carrots and celery in oil. Add broth and 2 cups water. Bring to a boil; simmer for 10 minutes. Stir in chicken, beans, tomatoes and seasonings. Reduce heat to low; cover and simmer for 25 to 30 minutes. Return to a boil; stir in pasta. Cook until pasta is tender, about 10 minutes. Add remaining water if soup is too thick. Stir in spinach and cook for 2 minutes, or until wilted. Makes 6 servings.

Canned beans are handy, but dried beans are very inexpensive and come in even more varieties. Dried beans can be slow-cooked for 8 hours to overnight on low. Cover with water and add a teaspoon of baking soda. In the morning, drain well and use immediately, or cover and refrigerate for up to 3 days.

Hearty Soups & Fresh-Baked Breads

Rosemary-Sea Salt Bread

Matt McCurdy
Saint Petersburg, FL

After my girlfriend moved out of state, I needed to learn how to cook and bake! Having zero cooking skills, I looked for recipes even I could do. Through trial & error I came up with this delicious bread.

4 c. bread flour
3 to 4 t. vital wheat gluten flour
2 t. active dry yeast
2 T. fresh rosemary, chopped
    and divided

2 t. sea salt, divided
2 t. extra-virgin olive oil, divided
2 c. warm water
2 t. cornmeal

In a large bowl, combine flours, yeast, one tablespoon rosemary, one teaspoon salt and one teaspoon olive oil. Heat water until very warm, about 110 to 115 degrees; add to flour mixture. Stir together until well blended; cover with plastic wrap. To allow flavor to develop, let stand at room temperature for about one hour, then refrigerate overnight up to 4 days. Before baking, let bowl stand at room temperature for one hour. Turn out dough onto a lightly floured surface; give dough a stretch or two. Line a baking sheet with parchment paper; sprinkle with cornmeal. Shape dough into a round loaf and place on baking sheet. Combine remaining salt, olive oil and rosemary in a small bowl; brush over dough. Spritz a little water into preheated oven. Bake at 475 degrees for 30 minutes; reduce to 400 degrees and bake for 10 additional minutes. Remove loaf to a wire rack. Cool completely before slicing. Makes one loaf, about 12 servings.

The flavor of bread shared has no equal.

–Antoine de Saint-Exupery

Kansas Beef Stew

Diana Krol
Nickerson, KS

This spicy soup is especially good served with crusty cornbread.

1-1/4 lbs. stew beef cubes
2 T. olive oil
1/2 c. onion, chopped
1-1/2 t. garlic powder
1/4 t. pepper

1 c. water
10-oz. can diced tomatoes with
   green chiles
1 T. ground cumin
1 t. salt

In a deep skillet over medium heat, brown beef on all sides in oil.
Remove beef to a bowl. Add onion, garlic powder and pepper to skillet;
cook until onion is translucent. Drain. Return beef to skillet; add water.
Bring to a boil; reduce heat to low. Cover and simmer for one hour,
stirring occasionally. Stir in tomatoes with juice, cumin and salt.
Return stew to a boil and simmer an additional 30 minutes, or until
beef is very tender. Makes 4 servings.

Make biscuit toppers for bowls of thick, hearty soup or stew...
they're almost like individual pot pies. Separate jumbo
refrigerated biscuits, flatten them and bake according to
package directions, until golden. Top each soup bowl
with a biscuit and dig in!

Hearty Soups & Fresh-Baked Breads

Italian Lentil & Vegetable Stew
Eleanor Dionne
Beverly, MA

Growing up in an Italian family, we ate a lot of vegetable dishes. We called it "peasant food" and boy, was it yummy. My mom always made some kind of homemade stew or soup every Monday in the winter. This slow-cooker recipe is still a favorite of mine.

1-1/2 c. dried lentils, uncooked
3 c. water
2 c. marinara sauce
1-1/4 lbs. butternut squash, peeled and cut into 1-inch cubes
1/2 lb. green beans, trimmed and cut into 1-inch lengths
1 green pepper, cut into 1-inch squares
1 potato, peeled and cut into 1-inch cubes
3/4 c. onion, chopped
1 t. garlic, minced
1 T. olive oil

Combine lentils and water in a large slow cooker. Add remaining remaining ingredients except olive oil; stir. Cover and cook on low setting for 8 hours, or until lentils and vegetables are tender. At serving time, stir in olive oil; ladle into bowls. Makes 8 servings.

Inexpensive light olive oil is just fine for most cooking.
Save the extra-virgin olive oil for making salad dressings,
where its delicate flavor can be enjoyed.

Lorrie's 2-Bean Chili

Lorrie Haskell
Lyndeborough, NH

A few years ago, I was looking for a meatless chili to make in my slow cooker. I found a recipe that needed just a little tweaking, and this delicious chili was the result.

1/2 lb. mushrooms, chopped
1 onion, chopped
3 stalks celery, chopped
1 green pepper, chopped
1 red pepper, chopped
Optional: 1 jalapeño pepper,
   seeded and chopped
1 T. olive oil
4 cloves garlic, minced
2 t. ground cumin

1-1/2 t. dried oregano
28-oz. can diced tomatoes
16-oz. can red beans, drained
   and rinsed
16-oz. can black beans, drained
   and rinsed
1 carrot, peeled and chopped
1/2 c. barbecue sauce
1/2 c. water
1/4 t. chili powder

In a large skillet over medium heat, cook mushrooms, onion, celery and peppers in olive oil until tender. Add garlic, cumin and oregano; cook and stir for 2 to 3 minutes longer. Drain; transfer to a slow cooker. Stir in tomatoes with juice and remaining ingredients. Cover and cook on low setting for 8 hours. Makes 6 servings.

Two meals in one! Make a big pot of your family's favorite chili and serve half of it one night. Another night, reheat the remaining chili and spoon it over baked potatoes. Top with shredded cheese and dollops of sour cream, if you like. Yummy!

Hearty Soups & Fresh-Baked Breads

Sweet Avocado Muffins

Trysha Lynn Mapley
Palmer, AK

Do try this simple pleasure of a recipe! If you like banana bread, you will love these muffins...they're sweet, buttery and delicious. The chopped walnuts toast to perfection as the muffins bake.

2 c. all-purpose flour
1 t. baking powder
1 t. baking soda
1/2 t. sea salt
2 eggs
1 c. sugar

1/2 c. canola oil
1-1/2 c. very ripe avocado,
    halved, pitted and mashed
1 T. lime juice
1-1/4 t. vanilla extract
Optional: 1/2 c. chopped walnuts

In a large bowl, mix together flour, baking powder, baking soda and salt; set aside. In a separate bowl, beat eggs and sugar until fluffy; stir in oil, avocado, lime juice and vanilla. Add oil mixture to flour mixture; stir just until combined. Spoon batter into 12 paper-lined muffin cups, filling 2/3 full. Sprinkle with walnuts, if desired. Bake at 350 degrees for 15 to 20 minutes, until a toothpick inserted in center tests clean. Remove muffins to a wire rack; let cool. Makes one dozen.

Freeze fresh, mashed avocado to keep on hand for quick recipe use...handy to know when avocados are on sale. Just add 1/2 tablespoon of lemon or lime juice per avocado, mix well and store in a plastic zipping bag, making sure to press out all the air before sealing. Thaw in the refrigerator before using.

Tex-Mex Quinoa Stew

Amanda Fox
South Weber, UT

I created this slow-cooker recipe for my husband. I was determined to create something that he would love and was good for him too. Enjoy this hearty stew! My husband sure does, and he doesn't even know what quinoa is or that he's eating Greek yogurt!

1 lb. boneless, skinless chicken
    breasts
14-1/2 oz. can diced tomatoes,
    drained
11-oz. can corn
2 cloves garlic, minced

1 c. quinoa, uncooked
1-1/4 oz. pkg. taco seasoning
    mix
1/2 c. fat-free plain Greek yogurt
1 c. reduced-fat shredded
    Cheddar cheese

Place chicken in a slow cooker. Top with tomatoes, undrained corn, garlic, quinoa and taco seasoning. Cover and cook on low setting for about 7 hours, until chicken is very tender. Remove chicken to a plate. Using 2 forks, shred chicken and stir back into stew. Serve stew in bowls, topped with a dollop of yogurt and a sprinkle of cheese. Makes 8 servings.

Add a healthy whole grain to your meals! Quinoa is a delicious grain that's cooked like rice. It has a bitter-tasting natural coating, so rinse it well before cooking. Cook up a batch to sprinkle into soups, sauces and salads.

Hearty Soups & Fresh-Baked Breads

Miss Sallie's Light Cornbread

Mary Little
Franklin, TN

We have enjoyed this yummy bread for many years at family gatherings. The recipe was given to me by my first-grade teacher.

1/4 c. oil, divided	1-1/4 c. sugar
3 c. self-rising cornmeal	2 c. buttermilk
1 c. self-rising flour	1 c. milk

Divide oil between two 9"x5" loaf pans. Heat pans in a 375-degree oven for about 5 minutes; remove from oven. In a large bowl, mix together cornmeal, flour and sugar; set aside. Combine milks in a small bowl. Tilt pans to coat with oil; pour remaining oil from both pans into milk mixture. Add milk mixture to cornmeal mixture; stir well. Divide batter evenly between pans. Bake at 375 degrees for 55 minutes. Cool before slicing. Makes 2 loaves, about 16 servings.

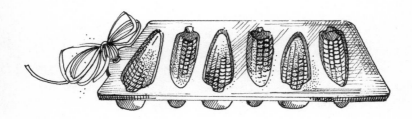

Just for fun, bake your next batch of cornbread in an old-fashioned corn stick pan...the kind that makes cornbread sticks shaped like ears of corn. Kids will love 'em!

Zucchini & Kielbasa Soup

Faye Phillips
Canton, OH

One year we grew a lot of zucchini, and I was stumped as to what to do with all of it. So I came up with this recipe...it has been a family favorite ever since! Serve in soup bowls with warm garlic bread or ladle it over cooked rice.

1 lb. Kielbasa sausage, sliced
    1/4-inch thick
1-3/4 c. water, divided
2 c. zucchini, thinly sliced
1 c. carrots, peeled and diced

1/2 c. onion, diced
28-oz. can crushed tomatoes
15-oz. can tomato sauce
garlic salt to taste

In a soup pot over medium heat, cook sausage until browned. Add a small amount of water to soup pot; scrape up brown bits in bottom of pot. Stir in remaining water and other ingredients. Cover and simmer, stirring occasionally, until zucchini and carrots are tender, about 30 minutes. Makes 6 servings.

When fresh tomatoes are out of season, canned tomatoes are often a better choice. Surprisingly, canned tomatoes actually have even more health benefits than fresh tomatoes. With a few cans of already-seasoned tomatoes in the pantry, you can whip up a flavorful meal anytime.

Hearty Soups & Fresh-Baked Breads

Cream of Celery Soup

Anna McMaster
Portland, OR

We love this smooth, comforting soup that uses potatoes instead of half-and-half for a creamy texture. Garnish each bowl with a few chopped celery leaves or a dash of paprika.

2 T. olive oil
1-1/2 c. onion, chopped
1 bunch celery with leaves,
   sliced
1 T. fresh thyme, chopped
1/2 t. salt
1/4 t. pepper

1/2 c. white wine or chicken
   broth
3 14-oz. cans chicken broth
2 c. water
3 russet potatoes, peeled
   and diced

Heat oil in a large saucepan over medium-low heat. Add onion, celery, thyme, salt and pepper. Cook for 20 to 25 minutes, stirring occasionally, until vegetables are soft and golden. Stir in wine or broth; simmer for several minutes, until liquid is nearly evaporated. Add broth, water and potatoes; bring to a boil over high heat. Reduce heat to low. Cover and simmer for 10 minutes, or until potatoes are very tender. Cool slightly. Use a hand-held immersion blender to purée vegetables in the saucepan; warm through. Makes 10 servings.

When a very smooth texture is desired, hot cream soups can be processed in a blender. Before you start, be sure to remove the center insert of the blender's lid, to avoid a "swoosh" of hot soup when processing.

Kristin's Peasant Stew

Kristin Stone
Little Elm, TX

I call this Peasant Stew because it's so easy on the budget!

1 eggplant, peeled and thickly sliced
salt to taste
2 T. olive oil
2 zucchini, halved lengthwise and thickly sliced

2 t. dried basil
1/4 t. garlic salt
4 c. chicken broth
1/2 c. elbow macaroni, uncooked
15-oz. can kidney beans, drained and rinsed

Sprinkle eggplant slices with salt on both sides. Let stand for 30 minutes; rinse well, drain and chop. Heat oil in a large stockpot over medium heat. Add eggplant, zucchini and seasonings; sauté until vegetables are crisp-tender. Add broth; bring to a boil. Stir in macaroni. Reduce heat and simmer for 10 minutes, or until macaroni is tender. Stir in beans; heat through. Makes 6 servings.

Bread bowls make a hearty soup extra special. Cut the tops off round bread loaves and hollow out, then rub with olive oil and garlic. Slip into the oven for 10 minutes at 400 degrees, until crusty and golden. Ladle in soup and serve right away.

Hearty Soups & Fresh-Baked Breads

No-Rise Whole-Wheat Bread

Suzanne Kresge
Lancaster, PA

When our sons were youngsters, they loved this simple bread with soups and casseroles. The loaves freeze well.

1 c. whole-wheat flour
1 c. white whole-wheat flour
1 T. sugar
1 t. baking soda
1/2 t. salt

1 c. buttermilk
1 egg, beaten
1/4 c. molasses
2 T. butter, melted

In a large bowl, mix flours, sugar, baking soda and salt. Add remaining ingredients except butter; stir well until moistened. Add butter; stir well. Turn batter into a well-greased one-quart round casserole dish. Bake at 350 degrees for 50 minutes, or until a toothpick inserted in the center comes out clean. Loaf will crack on top while baking. Set dish on a wire rack to cool for 10 minutes; turn out loaf and finish cooling on rack. Makes one loaf, about 8 servings.

When you're out of buttermilk, try an easy substitution.
For one cup buttermilk, add one tablespoon vinegar or lemon juice
to a measuring cup. Pour in enough milk to equal one cup and
let stand for 5 minutes...ready to use.

Daddy's Veggie Soup

Robyn Stroh
Calera, AL

One week my husband requested vegetable or cabbage soup. So I came up with this wonderful, veggie-packed soup that our daughter loves too. It makes plenty...tuck some in the freezer for a chilly day!

1 lb. extra-lean ground beef
2 onions, chopped
16-oz. pkg. baby carrots, cut
   into thirds
2 14-1/2 oz. cans green beans,
   drained

1 head cabbage, chopped
10-oz. pkg. frozen corn
2 46-oz. cans cocktail vegetable
   juice, divided
salt and pepper to taste

In a large Dutch oven over medium heat, brown beef with onions; drain. Add carrots. Reduce heat to medium-low; cover and cook for 10 to 15 minutes, until carrots are crisp-tender. Add beans, cabbage and corn; pour in one can vegetable juice. Increase heat slightly. Cover and simmer, stirring occasionally, for 30 minutes, or until cabbage has cooked down. Add remaining can of juice; continue to cook for 30 more minutes. Season to taste with salt and pepper. Makes 15 servings.

Do you love cabbage...but don't love the aroma? Keep your house sweet-smelling with this old-fashioned trick. Just add a lemon wedge, half an apple or a spoonful of vinegar to the cooking pot.

Hearty Soups & Fresh-Baked Breads

Hearty Potato Soup

Susan Willie
Ridgecrest, NC

I have been making this soup for many years, and my family loves it. It's easy to make and terrific on those cool, crisp autumn days.

6 potatoes, peeled and cubed
3 carrots, peeled and diced
3 stalks celery, diced
8 c. water
1 onion, chopped

6 T. butter
6 T. all-purpose flour
1 t. salt
1/2 t. pepper
1-1/2 c. milk

In a large soup kettle over medium-high heat, combine potatoes, carrots, celery and water. Cook until tender, about 20 minutes. Strain, reserving cooking liquid and setting aside vegetable mixture. In the same kettle over medium heat, sauté onion in butter until soft, about 5 minutes. Stir in flour, salt and pepper. Gradually add milk. Cook, stirring constantly, until thickened. Gently stir in cooked vegetables. Add one cup or more of reserved cooking liquid to bring soup to desired consistency; heat through. Makes 10 servings.

Save time when peeling and chopping veggies. Set a large bowl on the counter to toss all the peelings into...you'll only need to make one trip to the compost bin or wastebasket.

Fresh Gazpacho

Amanda Li
Brampton, Ontario

With a food processor or blender, you can make this refreshing cold soup in minutes! I like to use heirloom tomatoes when possible.

3 tomatoes, coarsely chopped
1 red pepper, coarsely chopped
1 English cucumber, peeled and
    coarsely chopped
1 c. fresh parsley or cilantro,
    coarsely chopped
1 clove garlic, minced
1 shallot, chopped

2 T. red wine vinegar or
    sherry vinegar
1 t. salt
1/2 t. cracked pepper
1 t. paprika
1/8 t. hot pepper sauce
1 to 3 T. water

Combine all ingredients except water in a food processor; process until puréed. Add water, one tablespoon at a time, to thin to desired consistency. For best flavor, cover and refrigerate for 2 hours before serving. Makes 6 servings.

Just for fun, serve gazpacho and other cold soups
in a margarita glass, garnished with a paper umbrella.

Hearty Soups &
Fresh-Baked Breads

Lemon-Rosemary Zucchini Bread

Lois Hobart
Stone Creek, OH

This zucchini bread is the best! It smells wonderful while it bakes and tastes so good. Mini loaves or muffins make a nice gift.

3 c. all-purpose flour
1/2 t. baking powder
2 t. baking soda
2 T. fresh rosemary, minced
2 eggs
1-1/4 c. sugar

1/2 c. butter, melted and
   slightly cooled
1/4 c. olive oil
1 T. lemon zest
3 c. zucchini, grated

In a bowl, whisk together flour, baking powder, baking soda and rosemary; set aside. In a separate large bowl, beat eggs until frothy; beat in sugar, melted butter and olive oil. Stir in lemon zest and zucchini. Add flour mixture to egg mixture; stir until blended. Divide batter into two 9"x4" loaf pans sprayed with non-stick vegetable spray. Bake at 350 degrees for 45 to 50 minutes. May also spoon batter into 24 paper-lined muffin cups, filling 2/3 full; bake at 350 degrees for 20 minutes. Makes 2 loaves or 2 dozen muffins, about 24 servings.

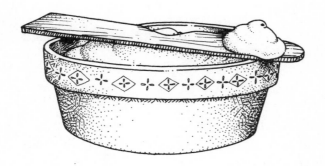

For an old-fashioned treat, make your own butter. Pour a pint of heavy cream into a chilled wide-mouth jar, cap the jar tightly and take turns shaking until butter begins to form. When it's done, uncap the jar and rinse the butter lightly with cool water. Spread on warm bread....delicious!

Chicken, Wild Rice & Mushroom Soup

Lyuba Brooke
Jacksonville, FL

A new twist on an old recipe I had for chicken rice soup. The wild rice gives it such a nice flavor! The recipe may seem lengthy at first glance, but it's mostly simmering time...perfect for a cozy weekend.

4 chicken breasts
9 c. water
3 cloves garlic, minced
3 T. butter
2 shallots, sliced

1-1/2 c. baby portabella
   mushrooms, sliced
8-oz. pkg. wild rice, uncooked
1/2 c. heavy cream or milk
salt and pepper to taste

Combine chicken and water in a large saucepan. Bring to a boil over medium-high heat; reduce heat to low. Cover and simmer for 60 to 90 minutes. Remove chicken to a bowl, reserving broth. Let chicken cool. Meanwhile, in a large stockpot over medium heat, sauté garlic in butter until fragrant. Add shallots and mushrooms; cook until almost tender. Add rice; cook and stir for 2 to 3 minutes. Add 7 cups reserved broth. Bring to a boil; reduce heat to medium-low. Cover and cook, stirring occasionally, for 20 minutes. Dice chicken, discarding skin and bones; add chicken to soup. Cover and simmer for 15 to 20 minutes, until most of broth is absorbed. If more liquid is needed, add remaining broth, one cup at a time, to desired consistency. Stir in cream or milk; bring to a boil. Reduce heat to medium-low and simmer for another 15 to 20 minutes. Makes 8 servings.

Use oversize mugs in an unexpected way...they're just the right size for servings of steamy soups, and the handle makes them so easy to hold on to.

Hearty Soups & Fresh-Baked Breads

Savory Apple-Cheese Bread

Sue Klapper
Muskego, WI

I serve this yummy bread for breakfast and at luncheons alongside soup or salad. It is a real favorite!

1/2 c. butter, softened
2/3 c. sugar
2 eggs
1 apple, peeled, cored
   and chopped
1/2 c. shredded Cheddar cheese

1/3 c. chopped walnuts
2 c. all-purpose flour
1 T. baking powder
1/2 t. baking soda
1/2 t. salt

In a large bowl, combine butter and sugar, beating until light and fluffy. Beat in eggs, one at a time. Stir in apple, cheese and walnuts. In a separate bowl, combine flour, baking powder, baking soda and salt. Gradually stir flour mixture into butter mixture. Pour batter into a greased 9"x5" loaf pan. Bake at 350 degrees for about one hour. Cool for 10 minutes; turn loaf out of pan onto a wire rack. Makes one loaf, about 10 servings.

An apple a day keeps the doctor away.
—Old saying

Spicy Chicken Soup

Stephanie Jenkins
McKinney, TX

This zesty, fresh soup is my husband's absolute favorite! When he was living in Guatemala as a missionary, I taught him how to make it, and he made it every week. Now, a bowl of this soup brings back fond memories of the trip I took to visit him there. If you want it spicier, add more jalapeños or some cayenne pepper.

1 lb. chicken breasts and/or
   thighs
1 onion, chopped
1 jalapeño pepper, seeded
   and minced
4 cloves garlic, minced
4 carrots, peeled and
   thinly sliced

8 c. water
salt and pepper to taste
3/4 c. brown rice, uncooked
Garnish: lime wedges, avocado
   slices, shredded Monterey
   Jack cheese

In a large soup pot over medium-high heat, combine all ingredients except rice and garnish. Bring to a boil; reduce heat to medium-low. Simmer, partially covered, for 45 minutes, or until chicken juices run clear. Remove chicken and set aside to cool, reserving broth in soup pot. Return broth to a boil; stir in rice. Reduce heat to low and simmer, covered, for 45 minutes, or until rice is tender. Meanwhile, shred chicken, discarding skin and bones. When rice is tender, return chicken to the pot and heat through. Serve soup in large bowls, garnished with a squeeze of lime juice, a few slices of avocado and a sprinkling of cheese. Makes 6 servings.

When slicing and chopping hot jalapeño peppers, it's a good idea to wear plastic gloves to avoid skin irritation. Be sure not to touch your face, lips or eyes while you're working! Afterwards, just toss away the gloves.

Hearty Soups & Fresh-Baked Breads

Sheila's Corn Soup

Suzanne Williams
Azusa, CA

When my daughter became a vegetarian, this was one of the first recipes she shared with me. It has become a family favorite. If you prefer, use evaporated milk or regular milk instead of the coconut milk. This soup freezes well...very handy when corn is fresh!

1/2 c. yellow onion, diced	sea salt and pepper to taste
1 T. olive oil	2 to 3 c. corn
5 cloves garlic, minced	14-oz. can vegetable broth
1 T. curry powder	14-oz. can coconut milk

In a large saucepan over medium-low heat, sauté onion in olive oil until tender, about 5 minutes. Add garlic and sauté until fragrant, 2 to 3 minutes. Stir in curry powder and season well with salt and pepper; cook another 2 to 3 minutes. Stir in corn, broth and milk. Cover and simmer over low heat for 25 minutes. With an immersion blender, purée soup to desired consistency. Makes 6 servings.

Enjoy the summery taste of fresh sweet corn year 'round...it's so simple! Remove husks; stack ears in a large pot and cover with water. Bring to a boil and cook for 5 minutes. Remove ears and chill in ice water until they're cool enough to handle. Cut the kernels from the cobs and store in freezer bags.

Chicken & Orzo Soup

Jen Thomas
Santa Rosa, CA

Fresh dill really makes this a chicken soup to remember.

1 T. olive oil
1 leek, halved lengthwise and
   sliced 1/2-inch thick
1 stalk celery, sliced
3/4 lb. boneless, skinless
   chicken thighs

6 c. low-sodium chicken broth
salt and pepper to taste
1/2 c. orzo pasta, uncooked
1/4 c. fresh dill, chopped
Garnish: lemon wedges

Heat oil in a large soup pot over medium heat. Add leek and celery; cook, stirring often, until vegetables are tender, 5 to 8 minutes. Add chicken and broth; season with salt and pepper. Bring to a boil; reduce heat to medium-low. Cover and simmer until chicken juices are no longer pink, about 15 to 20 minutes. Remove chicken to a plate, reserving broth in soup pot. Let chicken cool; chop. Meanwhile, return broth to a boil. Stir in orzo and cook until tender, about 8 minutes. Stir in chicken and dill; let stand several minutes, until heated through. Serve bowls of soup with lemon wedges for squeezing. Serves 4.

Cheer up a friend who's home with the sniffles. Fill a fabric-lined basket with a big jar of Chicken & Orzo Soup, some oyster crackers, a soup mug, a box of tissues and a cheerful book to read while recovering.

Hearty Soups & Fresh-Baked Breads

Cinnamon Apple-Raisin Muffins

Karen Jones
Baltimore, MD

These muffins are wonderful for breakfast and snacktime. I picked up this recipe at a farmers' market and added some tweaks to make it healthier. They freeze well.

1 c. all-purpose flour
1 c. whole-wheat flour
3/4 t. baking soda
1/2 t. salt
1 t. cinnamon
3/4 c. unsweetened applesauce
1/4 c. oil
1 c. sugar

1 egg, beaten
1/4 c. egg white substitute
1 t. vanilla extract
2 c. apples, peeled, cored
   and diced
1 c. raisins
1/2 c. chopped walnuts

In a bowl, stir together flours, baking soda, salt and cinnamon; set aside. In a separate large bowl, beat applesauce, oil and sugar with an electric mixer on low speed for 2 minutes. Add egg, egg white substitute and vanilla; beat for one minute and set aside. Add flour mixture to applesauce mixture; stir just until moist. Fold in remaining ingredients. Spoon batter into 12 paper-lined muffin cups, filling 2/3 full. Bake at 400 degrees for 25 to 30 minutes, until a toothpick inserted in center tests clean. Remove muffins from tin to a wire rack; serve warm or cooled. Makes one dozen.

If a muffin recipe doesn't fill all the cups in your muffin tin, add some water to the empty cups. This allows the muffins to bake more evenly.

West African Chicken Soup

Wendy Reaume
Chatham, Ontario

I had a friend long ago who used to make this delicious soup with flavors of tomato, chicken and curry. Over the years I've continued to make my own version, and it's well-loved by all.

2 boneless, skinless chicken
    breasts, cubed
1 c. onion, chopped
1 T. garlic, minced
1 T. olive oil
1-1/2 t. curry powder

salt and pepper to taste
28-oz. can stewed tomatoes
3 c. chicken broth
3 T. creamy peanut butter
3 T. tomato paste

In a large saucepan over medium heat, combine chicken, onion, garlic and olive oil. Sauté until chicken is golden and juices run clear when pierced. Stir in seasonings; cook for another minute. Stir in tomatoes with juice and remaining ingredients. Reduce heat to low; cover and simmer for 10 to 15 minutes. Makes 6 servings.

Get up and get going...a daily walk will do you a world of good!
Make your dog your personal trainer and go exploring around
your neighborhood or a nearby park.

Hearty Soups & Fresh-Baked Breads

Sweet Potato-Apple Soup

Kelly Hughes
Gainesville, GA

This is a warming, sweet soup from your slow cooker that's perfect for cold weather! Top with cheese and serve with hot buttered rolls for a scrumptious and satisfying dinner.

2 lbs. sweet potatoes
1/4 c. water
1 apple, peeled, cored and thinly
  sliced
1/2 c. onion, finely chopped

1 stalk celery, chopped
4 c. low-sodium chicken or
  vegetable broth
salt and pepper to taste

Place unpeeled sweet potatoes in a 13"x9" baking pan; add water to pan. Cover with aluminum foil. Bake at 350 degrees for one hour. Remove from oven; let sweet potatoes cool and peel off skins. Transfer sweet potatoes to a slow cooker; stir in remaining ingredients. Cover and cook on low setting for 8 to 10 hours. Purée soup to desired consistency with an immersion blender, food processor or blender. Makes 6 servings.

Need a little snack while the soup is simmering? Slice up some fresh veggies and serve with this super-simple dip. Blend one cup sour cream or Greek yogurt, one cup cottage cheese, one finely sliced green onion and one packet dried vegetable soup mix.

Hearty Hamburger Stew

Judy Phelan
Macomb, IL

A comforting weeknight meal...and with just one pan,
clean-up will be a breeze!

1 lb. ground beef
1 onion, chopped
1/2 c. celery, chopped
5-1/2 c. tomato juice
1 c. water

1/2 c. pearled barley, uncooked
2 t. chili powder
1 t. salt
1/2 t. pepper

In a large saucepan over medium heat, cook beef, onion and celery until beef is no longer pink. Drain; stir in remaining ingredients. Bring to a boil; reduce heat to low. Cover and simmer, stirring occasionally, for 50 minutes, or until barley is tender. Makes 4 servings.

Homemade soup always tastes even better if made a day ahead and refrigerated overnight. It's a snap to skim any fat too...it will solidify on the surface and can easily be lifted off.

Hearty Soups & Fresh-Baked Breads

Mile-High Biscuits

Victoria Mitchel
Gettysburg, PA

Once you taste these biscuits, I'm sure you'll agree that they are wonderful. The secret to making tender biscuits is to work quickly, with as little hand contact as possible. Enjoy...everyone needs a good biscuit in their life!

2 c. all-purpose flour
4 t. baking powder
1/4 t. baking soda

3/4 t. salt
5 T. chilled butter, diced
1 c. buttermilk

Combine flour, baking powder, baking soda and salt in a food processor; add butter. Pulse just until mixture resembles coarse crumbs. Transfer mixture to a large bowl; add buttermilk. Stir until mixture begins to hold together. Turn out onto a lightly floured surface. Working quickly, knead until most of the dough sticks together. Pat out dough into a circle 1/2-inch thick. Cut with a biscuit cutter, quickly re-gathering dough until about 8 biscuits are cut. Arrange biscuits in a parchment paper-lined 13"x9" baking pan. Set pan on center oven rack. Bake at 450 degrees for about 10 minutes, until lightly golden. Serve warm. Makes about 8 servings.

Don't have a biscuit cutter handy? Use a glass tumbler or the open end of a clean, empty soup can to cut the dough.

Peanut Butter-Banana Muffins

Kathy Bizier-Collins
Brookfield, CT

I love peanut butter and bananas, so I tried these muffins and fell in love with them! They are so yummy. Drizzle some melted chocolate on top for an added treat, like I do.

2-1/3 c. all-purpose flour
1-1/2 t. baking powder
1 t. baking soda
1/4 t. salt
1/3 c. butter, softened

1/4 c. creamy peanut butter
1/2 c. sugar
2 eggs
1 c. milk
2 ripe bananas, mashed

Combine flour, baking powder, baking soda and salt in a bowl; set aside. In a separate large bowl, combine butter and peanut butter; beat with an electric mixer on low speed until smooth. Add sugar; beat until light and fluffy, about 3 minutes. Beat in eggs. Alternately beat in flour mixture, milk and bananas with mixer on low speed until blended. Spoon batter evenly into 18 paper-lined or greased muffin cups, filling 2/3 full. Bake at 400 degrees for 20 minutes, or until a toothpick inserted in center tests clean. Cool muffins in tins on a wire rack for 10 minutes; turn out muffins and cool completely. Makes about 1-1/2 dozen.

Enjoy the taste of fresh-baked muffins any time! Place muffins in a freezer bag and freeze. To warm, wrap muffins in aluminum foil and pop into a 300-degree oven for a few minutes.

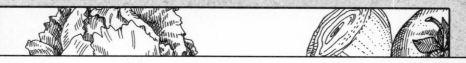

Garden-Fresh

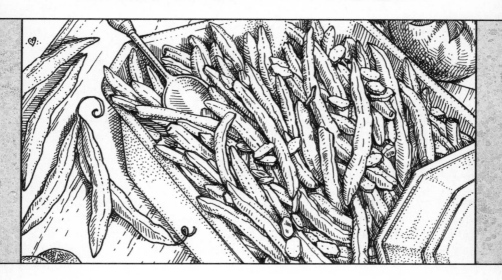

Sides &
Salads

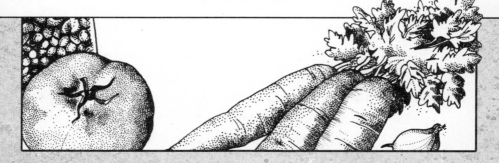

Cindy's Spinach & Corn Sauté

Cindy Katris
Franklin, OH

Here's a way to enjoy fresh spinach when it's abundant. You'll eat every bite even if you're not a fan of spinach! Enjoy with crusty French bread to soak up all the delicious drippings.

1 T. butter
1 T. olive oil
1 t. garlic, minced
1 bunch green onions, sliced
1 ear white corn, kernels cut
    from ear

1 lb. fresh spinach, torn
juice of 1/2 lemon
salt and cracked pepper to taste
1 tomato, diced
1/2 c. crumbled feta cheese

In a large skillet, melt butter over medium heat. Add olive oil, garlic and onions; sauté for 2 to 3 minutes. Stir in corn. Add spinach to skillet by handfuls; allow each handful to wilt slightly before adding more. Cook until spinach has reduced by half; remove from heat. Squeeze lemon juice over the top. Season generously with salt and pepper; top with tomato and cheese. Makes 6 servings.

Look for all kinds of delicious, nutritious fresh greens
at farmstands! Try spinach, kale, Swiss chard, collard greens,
bok choy, turnip greens, broccoli rabe or peppery mustard greens...
add to stir-fries, wilt in a hot skillet or just simmer
in broth with a little sautéed onion.

Garden-Fresh Sides & Salads

Gram's Zucchini in a Pan

Nancie Flynn
Bear Creek Township, PA

*Gram used to serve this as a main dish in late summer
when zucchini was plentiful. It's tasty as a side dish too.*

1/4 c. olive oil
1 onion, thinly sliced and
   separated into rings
4 to 5 sweet Italian peppers,
   sliced

2 zucchini, thinly sliced
2 tomatoes, diced
1 t. Italian seasoning
salt and pepper to taste
1 c. shredded Cheddar cheese

Heat olive oil in a skillet over medium heat. Add onion and peppers;
cover and cook until soft, about 5 minutes. Stir in zucchini, tomatoes
and seasonings. Cover and cook to desired tenderness. Remove from
heat; stir in cheese. Cover and let stand until cheese melts; serve
warm. Makes 6 servings.

Serve up a Southern-style vegetable plate for dinner. With two or
three scrumptious veggie dishes and a basket of buttery cornbread
or crunchy bread sticks, no one will miss the meat!

Arugula Potato Cornugula

Kelley Nicholson
Gooseberry Patch

A fast and easy recipe. Let your kids help you toss in the ingredients one by one, and with each ingredient come up with a silly word that rhymes with arugula. They're sure to give this side dish a try!

2 T. butter
1 t. garlic, minced
6 new redskin potatoes, sliced
1 T. seafood seasoning

1 c. frozen corn
1/2 c. frozen lima beans
1 c. fresh arugula, torn
salt and pepper to taste

Melt butter in a large skillet over medium heat; cook garlic until tender. Stir in potatoes and seasoning. Cover and cook until tender, about 10 minutes, turning occasionally. Add corn and beans; cook until potatoes are tender, about 8 to 10 minutes. Season with salt and pepper. Add arugula; cover and let stand until arugula is wilted. Makes 4 servings.

Going to the farmers' market? It's nice to have a shopping list handy, but leave a bit of wiggle room for foods that might be at the market early, or something new you've never tried before. Trying new things is part of the fun of going to farmers' markets!

Garden-Fresh Sides & Salads

Mexican Roasted Cauliflower

Michelle Powell
Valley, AL

A tasty veggie side to serve with tacos or enchiladas. It's a tasty alternative to refried beans & rice that even my cauliflower-haters love.

1/4 c. olive oil
3 cloves garlic, minced
1 T. chili powder, or to taste
1/2 t. ground cumin
1 lb. cauliflower, cut into
    bite-size flowerets

1/4 c. fresh cilantro, chopped
juice of 1 lime
salt to taste

Mix oil, garlic and spices in a large bowl. Add cauliflower; toss to coat. Spread in an ungreased shallow roasting pan. Bake, uncovered, at 325 degrees for one hour and 15 minutes, stirring occasionally. Remove from oven. Drizzle with lime juice; sprinkle with cilantro and toss well. Serve warm. Makes 6 servings.

For the healthiest meals, choose from a rainbow of colors... red beets, orange sweet potatoes, yellow summer squash, dark green kale and Brussels sprouts, purple eggplant and blueberries. Even white cauliflower offers valuable nutrients...so fill your plate and eat up!

Rosemary-Braised Navy Beans

Lori Rosenberg
University Heights, OH

*The hearty texture and aroma of this recipe make it
an instant classic, especially on cold fall or winter nights.*

1 lb. dried navy beans
10 c. water
6 T. dried rosemary, divided
6 cloves garlic, divided
3-1/2 t. sea salt, divided
1/2 c. plus 1 T. extra-virgin
   olive oil, divided

1 roma tomato, diced
1/4 t. pepper to taste
1/4 c. fresh parsley, coarsely
   chopped

Cover beans with water; soak overnight. Drain; transfer to a Dutch
oven. Add 10 cups water, 3 tablespoons rosemary, 3 pressed garlic
cloves and 3 teaspoons salt. Bring to a boil over high heat. Reduce
heat to medium-low; cover and simmer until beans are tender, about
one hour. Drain, reserving cooking liquid. To beans in Dutch oven,
add 1-1/2 cups reserved liquid, 1/2 cup olive oil, tomato, pepper and
remaining rosemary and salt. Slice remaining garlic and add to beans.
Bake, uncovered, at 475 degrees for 15 to 20 minutes, until creamy.
Add parsley and some more of the cooking liquid if beans are too dry.
Season with additional salt and pepper; drizzle with remaining olive
oil. Makes 6 servings.

Keep tomatoes stored at room temperature for
the best fresh-from-the-garden taste.

Garden-Fresh
Sides & Salads

Jolene's Chickpea Medley

Jolene Koval
Thunder Bay, Ontario

This unusual salad goes together in jiffy! It's terrific for warm-weather meals grilled in the backyard.

15-oz. can garbanzo beans,
    drained and rinsed
1 red pepper, diced
1 c. kale, finely shredded

1 zucchini, shredded
1 ear corn, kernels cut off,
    or 1/2 c. frozen corn, thawed
1/2 c. Italian salad dressing

In a salad bowl, combine beans and vegetables. Drizzle with salad dressing; toss to mix. Let stand 15 minutes before serving to allow flavors to blend. Makes 4 servings.

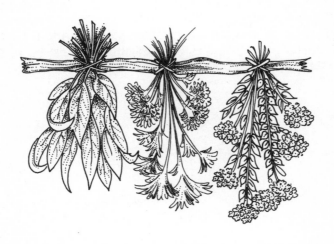

It's easy to dry fresh herbs...just bunch them together
with kitchen twine and hang upside-down in
a cool, dry place.

Sweet Potato Chili Wedges

Kathryn Harris
Valley Center, KS

I just love the sweet & savory flavor of chili powder on sweet potatoes. This is perfect as a side dish for either pork or chicken. I have even served it at Thanksgiving instead of a boring old sweet potato casserole. It will become a favorite of yours too.

2 lbs. sweet potatoes, cut into
   1-inch wedges
1 T. olive oil
1/2 t. salt
1/8 t. pepper

1/4 c. orange juice
1 T. honey
1-3/4 t. chili powder, divided
1/2 c. sour cream
1/4 c. fresh cilantro, snipped

Place sweet potato wedges in a large plastic zipping bag. Add olive oil, salt and pepper to bag; toss to coat. Arrange potato wedges in an ungreased 13"x9" baking pan. In a small bowl, combine orange juice, honey and 1-1/2 teaspoons chili powder; set aside. Bake, uncovered, at 450 degrees for 25 to 30 minutes, until tender, shaking pan occasionally and brushing 3 times with orange juice mixture. In a separate small bowl, combine sour cream, cilantro and remaining chili powder. Transfer potato wedges to a serving bowl. Serve with sour cream mixture for dipping. Makes 6 servings.

It's simple to substitute fresh baby spinach in recipes that call for frozen chopped spinach. Simply add 10 ounces of fresh spinach and 2 tablespoons water to a saucepan. Cook over medium-low heat for 3 minutes. Stir gently until wilted, then rinse in cold water, drain and squeeze dry.

Garden-Fresh Sides & Salads

Honey-Lime Peas

*Andrea Heyart
Aubrey, TX*

Peas prepared this way are one of the few green veggies that everyone in our family will eat! They're equally welcome whether served on Easter, the Fourth of July or Thanksgiving.

2 12-oz. pkgs. frozen peas
2 T. rice vinegar
2 T. honey
2 T. fresh chives, snipped
1 T. brown mustard
juice of 1 lime

1/2 t. garlic powder
1/4 t. cayenne pepper
2 t. sea salt
1/2 t. pepper
1/4 c. extra-virgin olive oil

Cook peas according to package directions; drain and transfer to a serving bowl. Meanwhile, combine remaining ingredients except olive oil in a food processor or blender. Pulse to combine; slowly stream in olive oil and blend well. Drizzle mixture over cooked peas and toss to coat. May be served warm or chilled. Makes 8 servings.

Plant a vegetable garden with the kids...even picky eaters may be willing to sample veggies that they grew themselves! Some easy-to-grow favorites are carrots, sweet peas, radishes, green beans and all kinds of peppers.

Stewed Lentils with Tomatoes

JoAnn

A satisfying side dish that's packed with good-for-you ingredients. This recipe also makes a delicious soup...just add more broth to the desired consistency.

2 t. olive oil
2 c. yellow onions, diced
2 c. carrots, peeled and diced
3 cloves garlic, minced
28-oz. can whole plum tomatoes
1 c. dried French green lentils, uncooked

2 c. low-sodium chicken or vegetable broth
2 t. fresh thyme, chopped
2 t. curry powder
1/4 t. pepper
2 t. salt
1 T. red wine vinegar

Heat oil in a large saucepan over medium-low heat; add onions and carrots. Cook, stirring occasionally, for 8 to 10 minutes, until onions are lightly golden. Add garlic; cook for another minute. Meanwhile, pour tomatoes and their juice into a blender. Process until coarsely chopped; pour into onion mixture along with lentils, broth, thyme, curry powder and pepper. Bring to a boil. Reduce heat to low; cover and simmer for about 40 minutes, until lentils are tender. Remove from heat; cover and let stand for 10 minutes. At serving time, stir in salt and vinegar. Makes about 8 servings.

Dried beans are nutritious, inexpensive and come in lots of varieties...perfect for family meals.

Garden-Fresh
Sides & Salads

Garlic-Roasted Broccoli

Kristy Wells
Candler, FL

I've been making this dish for so long I'm not sure where the recipe originated, but even those who don't love broccoli like it. Roasting broccoli and garlic gives them a whole new flavor. Kinda nutty, kinda sweet...a little like the chef!

1 bunch broccoli
3 T. garlic, minced

2 to 3 T. extra-virgin olive oil
salt and pepper to taste

Trim off one inch of broccoli stalks; pare tough skin from stalks. Cut stalks into quarters or thirds; arrange on an ungreased baking sheet. Sprinkle broccoli with garlic; drizzle with olive oil and season with salt and pepper. Bake, uncovered, at 375 degrees until tender and golden, about 15 to 20 minutes. Makes 6 servings.

Watch for whimsical diner-style sectioned plates at tag sales. They're perfect for serving up dinner to picky eaters. The sections keep all the various foods separate...no more excuses!

Farmers' Market Green Beans

Hope Davenport
Portland, TX

Our daughter is not too crazy about vegetables but she will eat green beans. We are always trying new ways to prepare them. This dish is especially delicious made with garden-fresh ingredients.

8 slices bacon, chopped
5 green onions, chopped
1-3/4 lbs. fresh green beans,
    trimmed

1/4 c. water
salt and pepper to taste

In a skillet over medium heat, cook bacon until crisp. Remove bacon to a plate, reserving 2 tablespoons drippings in skillet. Over medium-high heat, sauté green onions in reserved drippings for about one minute. Meanwhile, place beans in a microwave-safe dish; add water. Cover with plastic wrap; microwave on high setting for 5 to 7 minutes, until tender. Drain; cover with ice water. Drain again. Add beans, salt and pepper to skillet; sauté for 3 minutes. Stir in crumbled bacon. Makes 5 servings.

Bacon drippings may be poured into a jar and kept in the fridge. Add a spoonful or two when cooking hashbrown potatoes, green beans or pan gravy for wonderful down-home flavor.

Garden-Fresh
Sides & Salads

Comforting Creamed Corn

Michelle Powell
Valley, AL

Greek yogurt adds creaminess and protein to this simple dish.

1 T. butter
4 c. corn, thawed if frozen
1/2 c. plain Greek yogurt

2 T. grated Parmesan cheese
1 t. dried basil

Melt butter in a non-stick skillet over medium heat; add corn. Cook for about 6 minutes, stirring occasionally, until tender. Reduce heat; stir in yogurt and cook for 4 minutes. Stir in cheese and basil just before serving. Makes 8 servings.

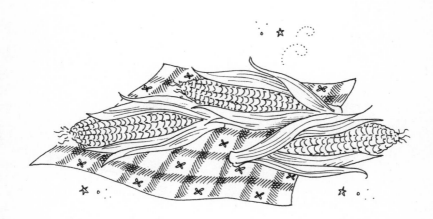

Make your own flavorful vegetable broth! Save up veggie scraps and trimmings in a freezer bag until the bag is full. Place the veggies in a soup pot, add water to cover and simmer gently for 30 minutes. Strain the broth and use it for homemade soup, or freeze it in ice cube trays to add extra flavor to soups and sauces.

Roasted Butternut Squash

Denise Piccirilli
Huber Heights, OH

I grew up eating all kinds of vegetables. Squash has always been a favorite of mine. I've served this savory squash with roasted chicken and mashed potatoes...delish!

4 c. butternut squash, halved
    and seeds removed
2 T. extra-virgin olive oil

1 T. fresh rosemary, snipped
2 t. kosher salt
1 t. pepper

Dice squash and spread on an ungreased baking sheet. Drizzle with olive oil; add seasonings and toss with your hands. Bake, uncovered, at 400 degrees for 30 to 40 minutes, until tender and golden, stirring once. Season with additional salt and pepper, if desired. Makes 4 servings.

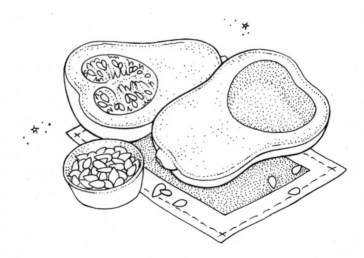

Butternut squash seeds can be toasted just like pumpkin seeds!
Rinse seeds and pat dry, then toss with olive oil and coarse salt.
Spread on an ungreased baking sheet and bake for 12 to
15 minutes at 350 degrees, until golden. Cool and enjoy.

Garden-Fresh Sides & Salads

Spicy Roasted Potatoes

Jen Stout
Blandon, PA

Mmm...potatoes seasoned with two kinds of mustard! This is a yummy, easy side dish. You don't even need to peel the potatoes.

2 baking potatoes, cut into
    1-inch cubes
1-1/2 t. dry mustard
1-1/2 t. Dijon mustard
1 t. olive oil

1 clove garlic, minced
1 t. dried tarragon
1/4 t. paprika
1/8 t. cayenne pepper

Place potatoes in a bowl; set aside. In a separate bowl, combine remaining ingredients; stir well and pour over potatoes. Toss potatoes until well coated. Arrange potatoes in a single layer on a lightly greased baking sheet. Bake, uncovered, at 425 degrees for 30 to 35 minutes, until tender and golden. Makes 4 servings.

Don't toss that nearly-empty Dijon mustard jar...mix up a zesty dressing! Add 3 tablespoons olive oil, 2 tablespoons cider vinegar and a clove of minced garlic to the jar. Replace the lid and shake well. Add salt and pepper to taste. Delicious drizzled over mixed salad greens and broiled fish.

Favorite Stir-Fried Zucchini

Marsha Pounds
Rolla, MO

Our garden produces lots of zucchini, and this is one of my favorite recipes for preparing it. It has been updated from a mid-1970s cookbook. My husband and I are trying to eat more a heart-healthy diet, so I decreased the amounts of fat and salt in the recipe.

1 T. olive oil
1 lb. zucchini, cut lengthwise
    into strips
1 onion, thinly sliced

1 T. sesame seed
1 T. soy sauce
1/4 t. sea salt

Heat oil in a large skillet over medium heat; add zucchini and onion. Cook for 5 to 10 minutes, stirring frequently, until crisp-tender. Quickly stir in sesame seed, soy sauce and salt. Heat through and serve promptly. Makes 4 servings.

The secret to tasty stir-fries:...cut everything into equal-size slices, strips or cubes before you start cooking! They'll all be cooked to perfection at the same time.

Garden-Fresh Sides & Salads

Lemon-Garlic Brussels Sprouts

Ann Mathis
Biscoe, AR

This has become a favorite to everyone in my family...
even the ones who said they didn't like Brussels sprouts!

1/4 c. olive oil
2 lbs. Brussels sprouts,
   trimmed and halved
5 cloves garlic, minced

zest and juice of 1 lemon
sea salt and pepper to taste
3 T. Gruyère cheese, grated

Heat oil in a large skillet over medium-high heat. Add Brussels sprouts; sauté for 7 to 8 minutes. Turn sprouts over; sprinkle with garlic. Continue cooking 7 to 8 minutes, until sprouts are golden, caramelized and tender. Reduce heat to low. Add remaining ingredients except cheese; stir to combine. Adjust seasonings, if needed. Top with cheese just before serving. Makes 6 servings.

Laughter really is the best medicine! Studies show
all kinds of health benefits come from time spent laughing...
it can even burn extra calories. So be sure to share funny
stories and even the kids' latest jokes everyday over dinner.

Sweet Potato Pancakes

Eleanor Dionne
Beverly, MA

We enjoy these for a change at dinner or even breakfast...they're just a little different from the traditional potato pancake!

1 c. sweet potato, peeled
    and grated
1 c. white potato, peeled
    and grated
1 t. salt, divided
1 c. carrots, peeled and grated
2 T. onion, grated
4 eggs, beaten

1/3 c. all-purpose flour
1/4 c. fresh parsley, chopped
juice of 1/2 lemon
pepper to taste
1/8 t. nutmeg
3 T. plain Greek yogurt
    or sour cream
1 T. fresh chives, snipped

Place potatoes in a colander over a bowl. Sprinkle with 1/2 teaspoon salt; let stand for 15 minutes. Rinse well; squeeze out well to remove all the excess water. In a large bowl, combine potatoes with carrots, onion, eggs, flour, parsley, lemon juice, seasonings and remaining salt. Mix well and form into 8 pancakes. Cook on a lightly greased griddle over medium-high heat until crisp and golden on both sides. Serve pancakes topped with a dollop of yogurt or sour cream and a sprinkle of chives. Makes 4 servings of 2 pancakes each.

Find an old-fashioned chalkboard to announce "Today's Special."
It adds a whimsical diner feel hanging in the kitchen and
lets the whole family know what's for dinner.

Garden-Fresh
Sides & Salads

Lori's Tater Wedges

Lori Peterson
Effingham, KS

This is a healthy substitute for French fries that we enjoy quite a bit with hamburgers on the grill. We always leave the skins on the potatoes, but peel them first, if you prefer.

4 baking potatoes, cut into
    8 wedges each
1 T. olive oil
1/8 t. salt

1/4 t. pepper
Optional: favorite seasoning
    blend to taste

Place potato wedges in a large bowl. Drizzle with olive oil and sprinkle with seasonings; toss until evenly coated. Arrange potato wedges in a single layer on a baking sheet sprayed with non-stick vegetable spray. Bake, uncovered, at 425 degrees for 30 minutes; turn over with a spatula. Bake an additional 30 minutes, until golden. Makes 4 servings.

No-Salt Seasoning

Barb Rudyk
Vermilion, Alberta

A tasty all-around salt-free seasoning to use on everything from meat to vegetables. Adjust the amounts to suit your family's taste.

1 T. garlic powder
1 T. onion powder
1 T. dry mustard
1 T. paprika

1 t. dried thyme
1 t. dried basil
1 t. cayenne pepper, or to taste
1/2 t. pepper

Mix together all ingredients and place in a shaker jar. Makes about 5 tablespoons.

Micky's Crunchy Sweet-and-Sour Slaw

Rosalind Dickinson
Grandview, WA

A family friend came up with this quick & easy summer salad one night when he and my hubby were barbecuing together. Since then, it's become a favorite. My sorority sisters have even requested my husband to make it for our get-togethers.

16-oz. pkg. shredded coleslaw
   mix
16-oz. pkg. shredded broccoli-
   carrot coleslaw mix
1-1/2 c. light or regular
   mayonnaise

1/2 c. cider vinegar, or to taste
1 T. garlic salt
pepper to taste
1 c. tomato, diced

Toss together coleslaw mixes in a serving bowl; set aside. In a small bowl, stir together remaining ingredients except tomato. Add to coleslaw mixture and toss to coat well. Gently fold in tomato. Serve immediately, or cover and refrigerate until serving time. Makes 12 servings.

For a refreshing, healthy beverage, ice-cold tea can't be beat! Fill up a 2-quart pitcher with water and drop in 6 to 8 of your favorite tea bags. Refrigerate overnight. Discard tea bags and add sugar to taste; serve over ice.

Garden-Fresh Sides & Salads

Citrus & Beet Spinach Salad
Stephanie Pulkownik
South Milwaukee, WI

This colorful salad is festive enough for celebration gatherings like graduations and confirmations, yet simple enough for everyday meals. It's delicious made with pecans and poppy seed dressing too.

10-oz. pkg. baby spinach
2-1/2 c. beets, cooked, peeled and diced
2 oranges, sectioned and seeds removed, or 11-oz. can mandarin oranges, drained

1/2 c. red onion, thinly sliced
1/3 c. chopped walnuts, toasted
1/2 c. raspberry vinaigrette salad dressing

In a large salad bowl, combine all ingredients except salad dressing. Add salad dressing immediately before serving; toss again and serve. Makes 8 servings.

To preserve the beautiful color and tasty flavor of beets, don't peel or slice them before boiling. Simply trim off an inch of the stem and root ends. After cooking, run the beets under cold water and simply rub off the skins with a paper towel...done!

Figure-Friendly 3-Bean Salad

Carol Jacobs
Anaheim, CA

Serve this flavorful salad in a chilled bowl...perfect for family meals and potlucks anytime.

2 14-1/2 oz. cans green beans, drained
14-1/2 oz. can yellow wax beans, drained
15-oz. can garbanzo beans, drained and rinsed
1 sweet onion, diced
1 green pepper, diced
1 red or yellow pepper, diced
1/4 c. balsamic vinegar
1/4 c. red wine vinegar
1/4 c. lemon juice
1/4 c. extra-virgin olive oil
4 to 5 envs. calorie-free powdered sweetener
salt and pepper to taste

Combine all beans and vegetables in a large serving bowl; set aside. In a separate bowl, whisk together remaining ingredients. Pour over vegetable mixture; toss to coat. Cover and chill; stir again at serving time. Makes 8 servings.

A nickel's worth of goulash beats
a five-dollar can of vitamins.
–Martin H. Fischer

Garden-Fresh Sides & Salads

Minted Tomato-Cucumber Salad

Karen Antonides
Gahanna, OH

I love making this refreshing salad in the summertime...fresh mint really makes it burst with flavor! It's terrific with grilled food and keeps well in the fridge.

1/3 c. white balsamic vinegar
1 T. sugar
1 t. salt
pepper to taste
2 cucumbers, cubed

1 pt. cherry tomatoes, halved
1/2 c. red onion, chopped
1/2 c. fresh mint, chopped
2 T. olive oil

In a large serving bowl, stir together vinegar, sugar, salt and pepper. Add cucumbers; toss to coat. Cover and refrigerate for one hour, stirring occasionally. Add remaining ingredients; toss gently. Season with additional salt and pepper, if desired. Makes 8 servings.

Try just one new herb at a time...a terrific way to learn which flavors you like. Some tried & true go-withs are ripe tomatoes and basil, sweet corn and chives, cucumbers and mint, potatoes and rosemary.

Zesty White Bean Salad

Amy Hunt
Traphill, NC

This tasty bean salad goes with anything! Try spooning it into toasted wonton cups for an easy appetizer too.

15-oz. can cannellini beans,
    drained and rinsed
1 tomato, diced
1/2 c. Kalamata olives, sliced
1/2 c. onion, diced

1/2 c. fresh basil, chopped
1 t. garlic, minced
1/3 c. sun-dried tomato
    vinaigrette salad dressing
salt and pepper to taste

Combine all ingredients in a large serving bowl; toss to mix. Cover and refrigerate until serving time. Makes 6 servings.

Cucumber-Mint Agua Fresca

Lisa McClelland
Columbus, OH

On a trip to Mexico, I was served this beverage one hot day. It's very refreshing...a great way to use up cucumbers and mint!

1 lb. cucumbers, cubed
6 c. water, divided
1/4 c. fresh mint, chopped
1/2 c. sugar

2 T. lime juice
ice cubes
Garnish: fresh mint sprigs,
    cucumber slices

Combine cucumbers, 2 cups water and mint in a blender. Process until puréed. Let stand in blender for 5 minutes to steep. Strain purée into a 2-quart pitcher. Add remaining water, sugar, lime juice and ice. Stir to combine; add more sugar, if desired. Divide evenly into 4 tall glasses; garnish as desired. Serve immediately. Makes 4 servings.

Add sprigs of fresh mint to ice cube trays before freezing.
So refreshing in a tall glass of lemonade or ice water!

Garden-Fresh Sides & Salads

Easy Tri-Color Bean Dish

Eri Niska
Fort Wayne, IN

*I came up with this recipe while looking in my pantry trying to
come up with a quick side dish for dinner. The result was
so yummy that I've made it over & over again.*

15-oz. can cannellini beans,
    drained and rinsed
12-oz. jar fire-roasted red
  peppers, drained and diced

12-oz. jar marinated artichokes

In a saucepan over medium-low heat, combine beans, peppers and
undrained artichokes. Gently heat through for about 5 minutes, until
artichoke marinade is absorbed by beans and peppers. Serve warm, or
cover and refrigerate for up to a week. Flavor will improve with time.
May be reheated before serving, just until warm. Makes 5 servings.

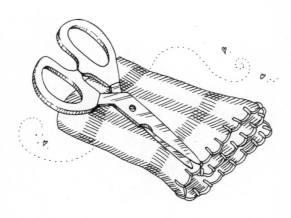

Kitchen shears are so handy for snipping fresh herbs,
cutting stewed tomatoes right in the can and snipping
the ends off fresh green beans. Just remember to wash them
with soap and water after each use.

Tomato & Mozzarella Salad

Ann Mathis
Biscoe, AR

You'll love all the fresh ingredients in this salad. Serve it with crusty bread and creamery butter for a wonderful light meal.

1 pt. cherry tomatoes, halved
8-oz. pkg. mozzarella cheese
   balls, drained
1/2 c. fresh basil, sliced into
   thin strips
2 T. fresh parsley, snipped

1/4 c. lemon juice
1/4 c. olive oil
salt and pepper to taste
1 avocado, halved, pitted
   and diced

Combine tomatoes, cheese and herbs in a large salad bowl; set aside. In a small bowl, whisk together lemon juice, oil and seasonings. Pour over tomato mixture; toss to coat. Cover and refrigerate for one hour. Stir in avocado just before serving. Makes 6 servings.

English cucumbers are more uniformly shaped and have practically no seeds...a good choice for salads. If you choose the waxy American variety, be sure to peel away the skin and remove any tough seeds.

Garden-Fresh Sides & Salads

Shealeen's Black Bean Salad

Karen Congeni
Bath, OH

My friend Shealeen got this recipe from a friend who lives in Venezuela. I have modified it over the years. It's delicious and versatile, and I get requests for it everywhere I take it. It may be enjoyed as either a salad or a dip for crunchy tortilla chips.

3 15-oz. cans black beans,
      drained and rinsed
15-oz. can light red kidney
      beans, drained and rinsed
10-oz. pkg. frozen corn, thawed
1 red onion, chopped
3 to 4 jalapeño peppers, diced

3 to 4 cloves garlic, pressed
1/2 c. red wine vinegar
1/4 c. olive oil
1/2 t. ground cumin
salt and pepper to taste
1 bunch fresh cilantro, chopped

In a large serving bowl, mix together all ingredients. Cover and refrigerate until serving time. If making ahead of time, mix all ingredients except cilantro; sprinkle cilantro on top of salad. Just before serving, stir in cilantro. Will keep for several days in the refrigerator. Makes 15 servings.

When it's just too hot to cook, invite friends & neighbors over for a salad potluck. Everyone brings along their favorite salad to share, and you set up a table in a shady spot and serve up frosty pink lemonade!

Bacon & Spinach Salad

Linda Peterson
Mason, MI

My favorite spinach salad in a tasty sweet-and-sour dressing.

1/2 c. bacon, crisply cooked
   and crumbled
24-oz. pkg. fresh spinach, torn
8-oz. pkg. bean sprouts
8-oz. pkg. sliced mushrooms
1/2 c. olive oil

1/3 c. catsup
1/4 c. white vinegar
1/4 c. powdered calorie-free
   sweetener, or to taste
2 T. Worcestershire sauce
1/2 c. onion, minced

In a salad bowl, combine bacon, spinach, sprouts and mushrooms; set aside. Whisk together remaining ingredients in a separate bowl. Add to spinach mixture and toss to mix well. Serve immediately, or cover and chill. Makes 6 servings.

Prefer a meatless dinner salad? Substitute roasted, salted pecans for crispy bacon as a salad topping with a similar salty-smoky taste and crunch.

Garden-Fresh
Sides & Salads

Corn, Tomato & Black Bean Salad

Alissa Post
Dallas, TX

*This salad is one of our family's favorites! It uses fresh, simple
ingredients to make a colorful and delicious side dish or appetizer.
We love to scoop it up and eat it with tortilla chips.*

5 to 6 ears corn, husked
2 15-oz. can black beans,
   drained and rinsed
6 green onions, green part only,
   chopped
1/2 to 1 red pepper, finely
   chopped

3 roma tomatoes, finely chopped
1 jalapeño pepper, seeded and
   very finely chopped
1 c. Italian salad dressing
garlic salt, salt and pepper
   to taste

Bring a large pot of water to a boil over high heat; add corn. Cook 4 for
6 minutes, just until tender. Drain; cool completely. Cut kernels from
cob to measure 4 to 5 cups. Place corn in a large serving bowl. Add
remaining ingredients and mix well, adding seasonings lightly. Cover
and refrigerate for 8 hours to overnight. At serving time, add more salt,
pepper, and/or salad dressing if needed. Makes 12 servings.

Lacy cheese crisps are a tasty garnish for salads and soups.
Sprinkle tablespoonfuls of freshly shredded Parmesan cheese,
4 inches apart, onto a baking sheet lined with parchment paper.
Bake for 5 to 7 minutes at 400 degrees, until melted
and golden. Cool and serve.

Apple-Pomegranate Salad

Wendy Ball
Battle Creek, MI

Whenever I make this recipe, it brings back memories of my grandparents, who were fruit growers in California. When the crops came in, they would send us fresh-picked pomegranates and wonderful pecans. Preparing this salad really makes me appreciate all the memories I made with them when I was growing up.

1 apple, peeled, cored and diced
juice of 1/2 lemon
1 head romaine lettuce, torn
seeds of 1 pomegranate
1/2 c. chopped pecans
2 T. champagne vinegar or
    white wine vinegar

2 T. canola oil
2 to 3 T. sugar
1/8 t. salt
1/2 c. shredded Parmesan
    cheese

In a small bowl, toss apple with lemon juice. Let stand for several minutes; rinse apple and pat dry. In a large serving bowl, combine apple, lettuce, pomegranate seeds and nuts. In a small jar, combine vinegar, oil, sugar and salt. Cover jar and shake thoroughly to mix; pour over salad. Toss until lettuce is completely coated; sprinkle with cheese. Makes 6 servings.

Baffled by the best way to extract the juicy seeds from a pomegranate? Simply cut the pomegranate in half and tap with a wooden spoon over a bowl until the seeds fall out. Be sure to discard all of the bitter-tasting white membrane.

Garden-Fresh Sides & Salads

Arugula & Nectarine Salad

Rita Miller
Lincolnwood, IL

*You'll love this fruity, nutty salad that's topped with
a fresh vinaigrette dressing.*

1/4 c. balsamic vinegar
1 T. Dijon mustard
1 T. honey
1/4 t. salt
pepper to taste
2/3 c. extra-virgin olive oil

1/4 lb. fresh arugula, torn
2 ripe nectarines, halved, pitted
   and sliced
3/4 c. chopped walnuts
1/2 c. crumbled feta cheese

Combine vinegar, mustard, honey, salt and pepper in a shaker jar. Add oil; shake until blended. Divide arugula among 4 salad plates; arrange nectarine slices over arugula. Sprinkle with walnuts and cheese; drizzle with salad dressing to taste. Makes 4 servings.

Nuts and seeds add fiber plus crunch and flavor too! Sprinkle sunflower kernels over tossed salads...stir sliced almonds or chopped walnuts into quick breads and cereals.

Hearty Greek Salad

Kathy Farrell
Rochester, NY

This is such an easy recipe! It's simple to make substitutions too, use any kind of olives or peppers you prefer. Terrific with crunchy bread sticks.

2 c. lettuce, shredded
1 c. cherry tomatoes, halved
1 cucumber, diced
1 green pepper, diced
1 red onion, diced
1/2 c. black or green olives, drained

1 T. red wine vinegar
2 T. lemon juice
3 T. extra-virgin olive oil
1/4 t. dried oregano
salt and pepper to taste
1/3 c. crumbled feta cheese or shredded mozzarella cheese

In a large serving bowl, combine lettuce, tomatoes, cucumbers, pepper, onion and olives. In a separate bowl, whisk together remaining ingredients except cheese. Pour dressing over lettuce mixture; toss well. Top with cheese and gently toss again. Makes 4 servings.

Large bottles of olive oil stay freshest when kept in the refrigerator. Pour a little into a small squeeze bottle to keep in the cupboard for everyday use.

Garden-Fresh Sides & Salads

Tomatoes in Red Wine Vinegar

Lori Bradbury
Redding, CA

A fabulous way to enjoy just-picked tomatoes!

4 tomatoes, sliced
2 green peppers, thinly sliced
   into rings
1/2 c. red onion, chopped

2 T. red wine vinegar
2 T. sugar
1/2 t. salt
1/2 t. pepper

Combine tomatoes, peppers and onion in a serving bowl; toss gently and set aside. In a separate small bowl, combine remaining ingredients. Stir well and pour over vegetables; toss gently. Cover and refrigerate for 8 to 10 hours. At serving time, drain. Makes 8 servings.

Mix up some herbal vinegar. Fill a Mason jar with a cup of finely chopped fresh herbs like parsley, chives, basil and dill. Pour in 2 cups white wine vinegar, heated just to boiling. Cap the jar and let steep, shaking it gently now and then. Strain vinegar after 3 weeks and use it to jazz up salads and deli sandwiches.

Barley Confetti Salad

Molly Ebert
Decatur, IN

*My wonderful son-in-law is vegan. That has challenged me
to come up with some new veggie dishes to serve when
he comes to visit. This salad with its bold flavors is a big hit!*

4 c. cooked barley
1/4 c. olive oil
3 T. lemon juice
2 cloves garlic, minced
1/2 c. fresh dill, chopped

2 c. tomatoes, diced
2 c. cucumbers, diced
1/2 c. green onions, sliced
salt and pepper to taste

In a large serving bowl, toss barley with olive oil, lemon juice and
garlic. Stir in dill. Add tomatoes, cucumbers and green onions; mix
gently. Season with salt and pepper. Cover and chill at least one hour
to allow flavors to blend. Makes 8 servings.

For satisfying warm side dishes and cool salads, try
whole grains like barley and brown rice. They're high
in protein and, with the addition of different seasonings, adapt
readily to many tasty flavors.

Chicken,
Pork & Beef

Mains

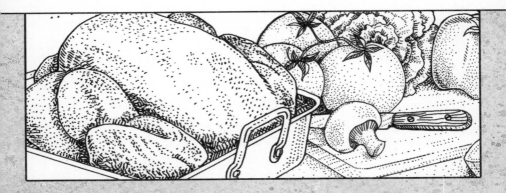

Honey-Lime Chicken

Liz Plotnick-Snay
Gooseberry Patch

*This chicken is full of flavor and wonderful served with
your favorite vegetable...we love it with steamed broccoli.*

4 boneless, skinless chicken
    breasts
zest and juice of 1 lime
1 T. honey

1 T. olive oil
1 T. fresh thyme, chopped
1 clove garlic, chopped
pepper to taste

Arrange chicken in a lightly greased shallow roasting pan; set aside.
Whisk together remaining ingredients except pepper in a small bowl.
Drizzle mixture evenly over chicken; season with pepper. Bake,
uncovered, at 375 degrees for 35 to 40 minutes, basting every
10 minutes with pan juices, until chicken juices run clear when
thickest part is pierced. Makes 4 servings.

Perfect portions! Fill half of each plate with colorful fruits
and/or vegetables. Add a grain like rice, pasta, barley or quinoa
to one-quarter of the plate and fill the rest with meat,
fish or other lean protein. With a serving of low-fat milk
or yogurt, you're all set for a healthy meal.

Chicken, Pork &
Beef Mains

Orange-Rosemary Glazed
Chicken

Cindy Jamieson
Barrie, Ontario

I had lots of clementine oranges that I needed to use up, but the kids were tired of eating them. So I decided to zest a few, juice them all and make this flavorful chicken...yummy!

1-1/2 lbs. chicken thighs	1 T. fresh rosemary, chopped,
1 c. orange juice	or 1-1/2 t. dried rosemary
1/2 c. balsamic vinegar	1/8 t. sea salt
2 T. brown sugar, packed	1/4 t. cracked pepper

Place chicken in a large plastic zipping bag; set aside. In a bowl or large measuring cup, whisk together remaining ingredients. Pour 3/4 of marinade over chicken; turn to coat. Close bag and set in a large dish; refrigerate for 4 to 6 hours, turning bag occasionally. Refrigerate remaining marinade separately. One hour before serving, remove chicken from bag; drain and discard marinade. Arrange chicken in an aluminum foil-lined 13"x9" baking pan. Bake, uncovered, at 400 degrees for 15 minutes. Reduce heat to 350 degrees; brush chicken with reserved marinade. Bake for an additional 30 minutes, or until chicken juices no longer run pink, brushing with marinade every 15 minutes. Let stand for 10 minutes before serving. Makes 4 servings.

Freezing extra pieces of chicken? Add a flavorful marinade to plastic zipping bags of uncooked chicken and freeze. When you thaw it for cooking, the chicken will be deliciously seasoned. So convenient!

Penne with Chicken & Snow Peas

Michelle Burke
Readlyn, IA

*This is my favorite quick-fix meal for busy nights with the kids'
school activities and a husband working the third shift. It may look
complicated, but it's really not difficult to boil the pasta, simmer the
chicken, make the sauce and steam the peas. I season the chicken
differently each time for lots of variety.*

16-oz. pkg. penne pasta,
   uncooked
1/2 c. grated Parmesan cheese,
   divided
6 boneless, skinless chicken
   breasts
2 T. olive oil

salt, pepper and Cajun seasoning
   to taste
1/4 c. butter, sliced
1 t. garlic, minced
2 c. whipping cream
8-oz. pkg. frozen snow peas in
   steamer bag, steamed

Cook pasta according to package directions; drain. Place in a large
serving bowl; sprinkle with 2 tablespoons cheese and set aside.
Meanwhile, brush chicken with olive oil and add seasonings. Add
chicken to a skillet sprayed with non-stick vegetable spray; cook over
medium heat until chicken is golden on both sides and juices no longer
run pink. To make sauce, melt butter with garlic in a deep saucepan
over low heat. Stir in cream and one tablespoon remaining cheese. Cook
and stir over medium heat until thickened, about 15 to 20 minutes,
adding a little more cheese to thicken if needed. Slice chicken and add
to pasta along with peas; pour sauce over mixture and toss to coat.
Sprinkle with remaining cheese. Makes 6 servings.

The most indispensible ingredient of all good home cooking...
love, for those you are cooking for.

–Sophia Loren

Chicken, Pork & Beef Mains

Basil Chicken & Tortellini

Kristin Stone
Little Elm, TX

This scrumptious dish evolved from a recipe my mother used to make. We love it...I hope your family will too!

2-1/2 c. cheese tortellini,
   uncooked
14-oz. pkg. frozen broccoli
   flowerets
3 boneless, skinless chicken
   breasts, cubed
1 t. garlic, minced
1/2 c. basil pesto sauce

1/4 c. white wine or chicken
   broth
2 T. lemon juice
2 T. water
1 T. plus 2 t. fresh basil,
   chopped
Optional: fresh basil sprigs

Cook pasta according to pasta package directions, adding broccoli along with pasta; drain. Meanwhile, spray a large non-stick skillet with non-stick vegetable spray. Over medium-high heat, cook chicken with garlic for about 2 minutes, until chicken is golden on all sides. Add remaining ingredients except basil sprigs to skillet, stirring to mix. Reduce heat to medium-low. Cover and simmer for 6 to 8 minutes, stirring occasionally, until chicken juices run clear. To serve, spoon chicken mixture over pasta and broccoli. Garnish with basil sprigs, if desired. Makes 6 servings.

Pasta dishes are easy to extend when you need to feed a few more people. Just add a little more pasta and a few more chopped veggies...no one will know the difference!

Phoebe's Asian Noodles

Gia Cecile Myers
Douglassville, PA

My teenage daughter Phoebe and I invented this recipe together one weeknight at home for an easy and somewhat exotic meal after a long day of work and school. This was both quick and delicious! We also enjoyed the chance to be creative together in the kitchen. This has now become a go-to favorite dinner!

8-oz. pkg. linguine pasta, uncooked
3/4 c. baby carrots, cut into thin strips
1/2 c. onion, thinly sliced
2 T. canola oil
1 lb. ground turkey
1/2 c. Asian sesame salad dressing
1 T. toasted sesame seed, divided

Cook pasta according to package directions. Drain; transfer to a serving dish and keep warm. Meanwhile, in a large skillet over medium-high heat, sauté carrots and onion in oil until softened, about 4 to 5 minutes. Remove vegetables to a plate; set aside. Brown turkey in skillet; stir in carrot mixture, salad dressing and 2 teaspoons sesame seed. Heat through; add to pasta and stir gently until combined. Sprinkle with remaining sesame seed. Makes 3 servings.

A super-simple, whimsical dessert to serve after an Asian meal!
Scoop rainbow sherbet into stemmed glasses, then slip
a fortune cookie over the edge of each glass.

Chicken, Pork &
Beef Mains

Beef & Snap Pea Stir-Fry

Sandra Sullivan
Aurora, CO

In a rush? Spice up tonight's dinner in 30 minutes with my go-to recipe for healthy in a hurry! Substitute chicken or pork for the beef, if you like.

1 c. long-cooking rice, uncooked
1 lb. beef sirloin steak, thinly
   sliced
1 T. cornstarch
salt and pepper to taste
2 t. canola oil
3/4 c. water
1 lb. sugar snap peas, trimmed

6 green onions, thinly sliced
   diagonally, white and
   green parts divided
1 T. fresh ginger, peeled
   and grated
1/2 t. red pepper flakes
2 T. lime juice

Cook rice according to package directions. Fluff with a fork; cover and set aside. Meanwhile, sprinkle beef with cornstarch, salt and pepper; toss to coat. Heat oil in a skillet over medium-high heat. Add half of beef and brown on both sides. Transfer to a plate; repeat with remaining beef. Stir in water, peas, white part of onions, ginger and red pepper flakes; season with salt and pepper. Cook until peas turn bright green, one to 2 minutes. Return beef to skillet; cook for another 2 to 3 minutes. Remove from heat. Stir in lime juice and green part of onions. Serve over rice. Makes 4 servings.

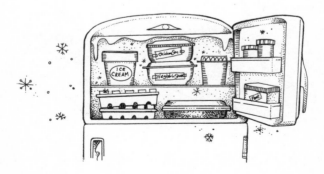

It's a snap to slice uncooked meat for stir-frying when it is slightly frozen...pop it in the freezer for 10 to 15 minutes before slicing.

Saucy Chicken & Green Beans

Kerri-Jo Sharp
Flackville, NY

We're a military family currently stationed in Germany. When I was pregnant with our son Michael, my husband Joshua came up with this recipe to satisfy a craving for Chinese food. Thanks, honey! Feel free to adjust the sauce amounts to your own taste.

4 boneless, skinless chicken
   breasts
1 clove garlic, sliced
1/3 c. teriyaki sauce

1 T. soy sauce
2 lbs. fresh green beans,
   trimmed

Place chicken on a lightly greased broiler pan. Broil until chicken is golden on both sides and juices run clear when pierced. Slice chicken into strips. In a wok or large skillet over medium heat, combine chicken and remaining ingredients. Cover and simmer until beans are crisp-tender, about 5 to 8 minutes. Makes 4 servings.

Sweet potato fries are deliciously different! Slice sweet potatoes into wedges, toss with olive oil and place on a baking sheet. Bake at 400 degrees for 20 to 30 minutes until crisp and tender, turning once. Sprinkle with a little cinnamon-sugar and serve warm.

Chicken, Pork & Beef Mains

Braised Pork & Peppers

Robin Hill
Rochester, NY

This savory dinner goes together in no time at all, and the colorful peppers look so festive. I like to serve it with cooked rice.

4 thick center-cut pork chops
salt and pepper
2 t. olive oil
1 T. tomato paste
1/2 c. onion, thinly sliced
1 yellow pepper, thinly sliced

1 red pepper, thinly sliced
4 cloves garlic, thinly sliced
1/2 t. dried thyme
1/2 c. white wine or chicken
  broth

Season pork chops with salt and pepper. Heat oil in a large skillet over medium heat. Brown chops on both sides, about 6 to 8 minutes total. Remove to a plate and set aside. Add tomato paste to drippings in skillet; cook and stir for 15 seconds. Add onion and peppers. Cook, stirring occasionally, until almost tender, about 3 minutes. Add garlic; cook and stir for one minute. Add thyme and wine or broth. Bring to a boil, scraping up browned bits in bottom of skillet. Return chops to skillet; reduce heat to medium-low. Cover and cook about 4 minutes; turn chops over. Cover and cook another 3 to 5 minutes, until chops are cooked through. Serve chops topped with vegetable mixture. Makes 4 servings.

Stem and seed a sweet pepper in a flash...hold the pepper upright on a cutting board. Use a sharp knife to slice each of the sides from the pepper. You'll then have four large seedless pieces that can easily be chopped.

Orchard Pork Chops

Nancy Wise
Little Rock, AR

My family loves to go to the U-pick orchard for ripe fruit...but sometimes we bring too much home! When there are extra plums or nectarines to use up, this is how I like to serve them.

4 thick pork shoulder chops
salt and pepper to taste
2 t. canola oil

1/2 c. yellow onion, diced
3 ripe plums, halved, pitted and
  cut into wedges

Season pork chops with salt and pepper. In a large skillet, heat oil over medium-high heat. Add chops; cook until golden on both sides and juices run clear, about 6 minutes. Remove to a plate and set aside. Add onion to drippings in skillet and cook until translucent, about 3 minutes. Add plums. Cook, stirring occasionally, for about 3 minutes, until plums begin to soften and onion is tender. Season onion mixture with additional salt and pepper. To serve, spoon onion mixture over chops. Makes 4 servings.

Try a new side dish instead of rice or noodles...barley pilaf. Simply prepare quick-cooking barley with chicken broth instead of water. Season with a little chopped onion and dried parsley. Filling, healthful and tasty!

Chicken, Pork & Beef Mains

Chicken & Snow Pea Stir-Fry

Jennie Gist
Gooseberry Patch

Delicious! Also try this recipe with beef sirloin instead of chicken, diced fresh tomatoes and even Japanese-style buckwheat noodles. Quick and satisfying.

8-oz. pkg. medium egg noodles, uncooked
3/4 c. orange juice
3 T. soy sauce
4 t. cornstarch
1 T. brown sugar, packed
1/2 t. ground ginger
1 lb. boneless, skinless chicken breast, thinly sliced
2 t. canola oil
14-1/2 oz. can diced tomatoes
2 c. snow peas, trimmed

Cook noodles according to package directions; drain. Meanwhile, in a small bowl, combine orange juice, soy sauce, cornstarch, brown sugar and ginger; mix well and set aside. In a wok or large skillet over medium-high heat, cook and stir chicken in oil for 2 minutes, or until golden. Drain; add orange juice mixture and tomatoes with juice to skillet. Cook and stir until mixture is thickened. Add snow peas; cook and stir for 2 minutes, or until crisp-tender. Serve chicken mixture over hot noodles. Makes 4 servings.

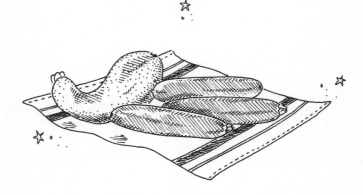

For a delicious low-calorie change from pasta, make "noodles" from zucchini or yellow squash. Cut into long, thin strips, steam lightly or sauté in a little olive oil and toss with your favorite sauce.

Spectacular Roast Chicken & Vegetables

Lisa Engwell
Bellevue, NE

A favorite comfort food dinner at our home. I've adapted it from a recipe found many years ago in a magazine, and my family just loves it. The aroma will put a smile on your face!

2 sweet potatoes, peeled and coarsely chopped
4 redskin potatoes, coarsely chopped
4 plum tomatoes, cut into wedges
1 green pepper, coarsely chopped

1/4 c. olive oil
4 t. seasoned salt
2 t. garlic pepper seasoning
2 t. dried basil
3-1/2 lbs. chicken, cut up

Combine vegetables in a bowl; set aside. Mix olive oil and seasonings in a small bowl; drizzle half of mixture over vegetables and toss to coat well. Spread vegetables on a lightly oiled 15"x10" jelly-roll pan. Arrange chicken pieces on top of vegetables; brush with remaining olive oil mixture. Bake, uncovered, at 400 degrees for 45 to 50 minutes, until vegetables are tender and chicken is crisp, golden and juices run clear. Makes 6 servings.

Make a double batch of your favorite comfort food and invite neighbors over for supper...what a great way to get to know them better. Keep it simple with a tossed salad, warm bakery bread and apple crisp for dessert. It's all about food and fellowship!

Chicken, Pork & Beef Mains

Mom's Chicken Paprikash

Nancy Bogart
Euclid, OH

My mom used to serve this quick & easy chicken dish...now it's a favorite in my home too! It is ready to serve in 30 minutes.

8-oz. pkg. wide egg noodles,
  uncooked
4 T. butter, divided
1 onion, thinly sliced
1 green or red pepper,
  thinly sliced
2 T. sweet paprika
2 cloves garlic, pressed

2 lbs. boneless, skinless chicken
  breast, cut into 2-inch cubes
1/2 t. salt
1/4 t. pepper
14-1/2 oz. can chicken broth
14-1/2 oz. can diced tomatoes
1 c. sour cream
Garnish: chopped fresh parsley

Cook egg noodles according to package directions; drain and set aside. Meanwhile, melt 2 tablespoons butter in a Dutch oven over medium heat. Add onion, green or red pepper, paprika and garlic; sauté until onion is soft and aromatic. Remove onion mixture to a bowl; cover and keep warm. Melt remaining butter in pan. Add chicken, salt and pepper; cook until golden on all sides. Return onion mixture to pan; add broth and tomatoes with juice. Cover and cook about 20 minutes, until chicken juices run clear when pierced. Reduce heat to low. Stir in noodles and sour cream; warm through. Serve garnished with parsley. Makes 6 servings.

Oven Chicken Fajitas

Diana Krol
Nickerson, KS

A quick & easy way to enjoy fajitas right at home...it's delicious!

1 lb. boneless, skinless chicken
   breasts, cut into strips
2 T. olive oil
1/4 t. salt
2 t. chili powder
2 t. ground cumin
1/2 t. garlic powder
1/2 t. dried oregano

1 onion, sliced
1 green pepper, sliced
10-oz. can diced tomatoes with
   green chiles
8 10-inch flour tortillas
Garnish: shredded cheese, sour
   cream, guacamole, sliced hot
   peppers, sliced green onions

Place chicken in a greased 13"x9" baking pan; set aside. In a small
bowl, mix oil and seasonings. Drizzle oil mixture over chicken; stir in
onion, green pepper and tomatoes with juice. Bake, uncovered, at
400 degrees for 25 to 30 minutes, until chicken juices run clear and
vegetables are tender. Serve chicken and vegetables wrapped in
tortillas and garnished as desired. Makes 8 servings.

Salsa in a jiffy! Pour a can of stewed tomatoes, several slices of
canned jalapeño pepper and a teaspoon or two of the jalapeño
juice into a blender. Cover and process to the desired consistency.

Chicken, Pork & Beef Mains

Chicken Mole Verde

Susana Rodriguez
Rialto, CA

This recipe reminds me of my grandmother, who has long since passed. She was a wonderful cook, and this is real comfort food. The tomatoes, garlic and pepper don't need to be chopped...just add them whole.

3-1/2 lbs. chicken, cut up
1/2 onion
3 cloves garlic, divided
1 T. chicken soup base
salt to taste
6 green tomatoes

1/2 green jalapeño pepper, seeds
   removed if desired
1/2 c. shelled pumpkin seeds
1/4 c. fresh cilantro, chopped
cooked Mexican rice

Place chicken in a stockpot; cover with water. Add onion, 2 cloves garlic, soup base and salt. Cook over medium-low heat until tender, 45 minutes to one hour. Drain, reserving one cup broth; return chicken to pot. Meanwhile, in a saucepan, cover tomatoes, jalapeño and remaining garlic clove with water. Cook over medium-high heat for 15 to 25 minutes, until tomatoes are soft and opaque green; drain. In a dry skillet over medium-high heat, toast pumpkin seeds until lightly golden, stirring often. Transfer tomato mixture, reserved broth, pumpkin seeds and cilantro into a blender. Process until smooth; add salt to taste. Spoon tomato mixture over chicken. Cover; simmer over low heat until warmed through. Serve with your favorite Mexican rice. Makes 6 servings.

Grandma's
Recipe
Collection

Take time to share family stories and traditions with
your kids over the dinner table. A cherished family recipe
can be a super conversation starter.

Bowties & Sausage

Cindy McKinnon
El Dorado, AR

*This quick & easy dish is one of my husband's favorites.
Other kinds of pasta like penne or ziti work well also. I like to
serve warm French bread with it.*

8-oz. pkg. bowtie pasta,
   uncooked
1 T. olive oil
1 lb. Italian pork sausage,
   cut into 1/2-inch pieces

1 green pepper, chopped
1 onion, chopped
1/2 c. beef broth
salt and pepper to taste

Cook pasta according to package directions, just until tender; drain.
Meanwhile, heat olive oil in a large skillet over medium heat. Add
sausage, green pepper and onion. Cook until sausage is no longer pink
and vegetables are tender; drain. Add broth to skillet; season with salt
and pepper. Bring to a boil; mix in cooked pasta and heat through.
Makes 4 servings.

If you often use chopped onion and green pepper to add flavor
to sautéed dishes, save time by chopping lots at once to
freeze in a plastic freezer container. Add it to skillet dishes
straight from the freezer...there's no need to thaw.

Chicken, Pork & Beef Mains

Pan-Fried Pork Chops

Angie Venable
Gooseberry Patch

*These pork chops are so tender and juicy! My family
loves this recipe and so will yours.*

8 thin-cut bone-in pork chops
2 t. seasoned salt
1 t. pepper
1 c. all-purpose flour

1 T. cayenne pepper
1/2 c. olive oil
1 T. butter, sliced

Sprinkle both sides of pork chops with seasoned salt and pepper.
Combine flour, cayenne pepper and additional salt and pepper to taste
in a shallow dish. Dredge chops in flour mixture on both sides; set
aside. Heat olive oil in a skillet over medium-high heat; stir in butter.
Add 2 to 3 chops and cook for 3 minutes on one side. Turn over;
cook other side until crisp, golden and juices run clear. Remove chops
to a serving plate; cover and keep warm. Repeat with remaining chops.
Makes 4 servings, 2 chops per serving.

Homemade applesauce is a natural partner for pork, and it's easy
to make. Peel, core and chop 4 tart apples and place in a saucepan
with 1/4 cup brown sugar, 1/4 cup water and 1/2 teaspoon
cinnamon. Cook over medium-low heat for 8 to 10 minutes,
until soft. Mash with a potato masher and serve warm.

South-of-the-Border Squash Skillet

Brenda Rogers
Atwood, CA

Our family grows lots of yellow summer squash in our community garden. We love tacos, so this taco-flavored recipe is a yummy way to use it up! If you omit the meat, it's also a great vegetarian dish.

1 lb. ground beef or turkey
1/3 c. onion, diced
1/3 c. water
1-1/4 oz. pkg. taco seasoning
   mix

4 to 5 yellow squash, zucchini
   or crookneck squash,
   chopped
1 c. shredded Cheddar cheese

In a skillet over medium heat, brown meat with onion; drain. Stir in water and taco seasoning; add squash. Cover and simmer for about 10 minutes, until squash is tender. Stir in cheese; cover and let stand just until cheese melts. Makes 4 servings.

A fresh tomato salad is a snap to prepare. Whisk together 1/4 cup white vinegar with one teaspoon chopped banana pepper and 3/4 teaspoon salt. Drizzle over one cup thinly sliced onion and 4 tomatoes cut into thin wedges. Let stand 15 minutes before serving.

Chicken, Pork & Beef Mains

Spicy Steak Tostadas

Joan Shaffer
Chambersburg, PA

I created this recipe for a quick lunch or supper. My family loves Mexican food, and this is a tasty change from tacos.

1 T. oil
1-1/2 lbs. beef sirloin steak,
   thinly sliced
2 onions, thinly sliced
1/2 red pepper, thinly sliced
1/2 yellow pepper, thinly sliced
1 clove garlic, minced

2 c. salsa
1 T. chili powder
1/2 t. ground cumin
6 corn tostadas
1 c. shredded Mexican-blend
   cheese

Heat oil in a large skillet over medium-high heat; add beef. Stir-fry until no longer pink; remove to a plate. Add onions, peppers and garlic to skillet; stir-fry until crisp-tender. Drain; return beef to skillet. Stir in salsa and spices. Reduce heat to low. Cover and simmer until thickened, stirring occasionally, about one hour. To serve, spoon beef mixture over tostadas; top with cheese. Makes 6 servings.

If your family loves spicy food, why not mix up your own chili powder blend? Fill a shaker with 2 teaspoons garlic powder, 2 teaspoons cumin and one teaspoon each of cayenne pepper, paprika and oregano. It's easy to adjust to your own taste.

Roasted Veggies & Kielbasa

Carrie Fostor
Baltic, OH

One of my favorite meals! We eat this simple and tasty dish year 'round, but especially look forward to it in the fall. It even makes a nice campfire meal...just place a little of each item in aluminum foil, wrap to seal and cook until the veggies are tender.

1 lb. Kielbasa sausage, sliced
    into bite-size pieces
6 potatoes, peeled and chopped
1 c. baby carrots

1 onion, halved and sliced
1 green pepper, cut into squares
8-oz. pkg. mushrooms, halved
Cajun seasoning to taste

Combine all ingredients in a roaster pan. For a moist consistency, cover before baking; leave uncovered for a dryer consistency. Bake at 425 degrees for 30 minutes, or until vegetables are tender. Makes 8 servings.

Cajun Seasoning

Teresa Moore
Pawhuska, OK

I got this wonderful seasoning recipe many years ago while working on a pipeline job. It's terrific on so many things like steaks, burgers, chicken, pork chops, casseroles, chili...you name it! It makes quite a bit, so I keep it in a vintage shaker on my stovetop.

16-oz. pkg. salt
2-oz. jar black pepper
2-oz. jar white pepper

2-oz. jar cayenne pepper
2-oz. jar chili powder
2-oz. jar garlic powder

Combine all ingredients in a large bowl; mix well. Store in a large shaker jar. Makes about 2-1/2 cups.

Chicken, Pork & Beef Mains

Italian Chicken & Pasta

Wendy Reaume
Chatham, Ontario

I used to make this dish back in my college years when my budget was really tight. Nutritious, cheap, easy, fast...and tasty! Comfort food doesn't get better than that.

8-oz. pkg. linguine pasta,
    uncooked
1/4 c. olive oil
4 boneless, skinless chicken
    breasts or thighs, cubed
1 onion, chopped

1 green pepper, chopped
1 clove garlic, pressed
1 T. balsamic vinegar
Garnish: shredded Parmesan
    cheese

Cook pasta according to package directions; drain. Meanwhile, heat oil in a large skillet over medium-high heat. Add chicken, onion, and pepper to skillet; sprinkle with Seasoning Mix, garlic and vinegar. Reduce heat to medium. Cook, stirring frequently and lightly scraping up brown bits from bottom of skillet. When chicken is golden and vegetables are soft, stir in pasta. Serve topped with Parmesan cheese. Makes 4 servings.

Seasoning Mix:

1/2 t. dried oregano
1/2 t. dried basil
1/2 t. red pepper flakes
1/4 t. fennel seed

1/4 t. dried marjoram
1/4 t. dried thyme
1/4 t. pepper

Mix all ingredients in a small bowl.

If you have a favorite busy-day recipe that calls for lots of different herbs or spices, measure them out into several small plastic zipping bags and label. Later, when time is short, just tip a bag into the cooking pot.

Chicken Cacciatore

Wendi Knowles
Pittsfield, ME

When I was 16 years old, this was the first recipe I made. I was making dinner for my boyfriend, who later became my husband. I didn't know all the cooking vocabulary then, and Mom cracked up laughing when she came in the kitchen to find me "patting" the chicken dry. I was just slapping it with my bare hands! Since then, I've learned to look up any instructions I may not understand.

3 lbs. chicken, cut up
1/2 c. all-purpose flour
1/4 c. olive oil
2 c. onion, thinly sliced
1/2 c. green pepper, sliced
2 cloves garlic, minced
1/4 c. red wine or chicken broth

15-oz. can diced tomatoes, drained
8-oz. can tomato sauce
4-oz. can sliced mushrooms, drained
1/4 t. dried oregano
1 t. salt

Pat chicken pieces dry; coat with flour. In a large skillet, heat oil over medium heat. Place chicken in skillet and cook for 15 to 20 minutes, until golden on both sides. Remove chicken to a plate; cover with aluminum foil and set aside. Add onion, green pepper and garlic to drippings in skillet; cook and stir until vegetables are tender. Add wine or broth, scraping up brown bits in bottom of skillet. Add remaining ingredients; stir until blended. Return chicken to skillet, spooning some of the sauce over chicken. Cover and cook for about one hour, until chicken is tender and juices run clear. Makes 6 servings.

Oops, the family's dinner plans have changed, and dinner is already thawing. No problem! As long as some ice crystals remain, it's perfectly safe to return partially defrosted food to the freezer.

Chicken, Pork & Beef Mains

Baked Pork Chops & Rice

Jeanne Allen
Menomonee Falls, WI

Country-style goodness...a perfect recipe for a cherished old cast-iron skillet.

6 lean pork chops
salt and pepper to taste
2 T. canola oil
1/2 c. onion, chopped
1/2 c. green pepper, chopped

1/2 c. celery, chopped
1 c. long-cooking rice, uncooked
2 c. chicken broth
1/2 t. dried thyme or sage

Season pork chops with salt and pepper; set aside. Heat oil over medium heat in a cast-iron or other oven-proof skillet. Add chops; brown on both sides. Drain; remove chops to a plate. Add onion, celery, green pepper and rice to skillet. Cook until vegetables are tender and rice is golden, stirring to loosen brown bits in bottom of skillet. Bring broth to a boil and add to skillet. Stir in thyme or sage. Place chops on top of rice mixture. Cover and bake at 350 degrees for 30 minutes, or until chops and rice are tender and liquid is absorbed. Makes 6 servings.

Goode & Healthy "Fried" Chicken

Cris Goode
Mooresville, IN

This very simple recipe gives you all the deliciousness of real fried chicken without all the fat and calories. Don't be fooled, though... we rarely have leftovers of this family favorite!

3 egg whites
2 to 3 c. panko bread crumbs

salt and pepper to taste
10 chicken thighs, skin removed

Beat egg whites in a shallow dish; set aside. Combine bread crumbs, salt and pepper in a gallon-size plastic zipping bag. Coat chicken with egg whites, one piece at a time. Drop chicken into bag and shake to coat lightly. Arrange chicken in two 13"x9" baking pans coated with non-stick vegetable spray. Bake, uncovered, at 350 degrees for 30 to 40 minutes, until chicken juices run clear. Makes 10 servings.

Salsa Verde Chicken & Biscuits

Anne Alesauskas
Minocqua, WI

This recipe is a winner...I love it! The sauce is so scrumptious that the biscuits are a must to soak up all that goodness.

1/4 c. butter, sliced
1/2 c. all-purpose flour
2 c. chicken broth
16-oz. jar salsa verde
5-oz. can fat-free evaporated
    milk

1-1/2 lbs. boneless, skinless
    chicken breasts, cooked
    and diced
2 c. biscuit baking mix
2/3 c. milk
3/4 c. shredded Cheddar cheese

In a large saucepan, melt butter over medium-high heat. Whisk in flour; cook and stir for 2 minutes. Add broth, salsa and evaporated milk; continue to cook and stir until thick and bubbly. Stir in chicken; reduce heat to low. Meanwhile, in a bowl, combine biscuit mix, milk and cheese. Pour chicken mixture into a lightly greased 13"x9" baking pan. Top with large spoonfuls of biscuit dough. Bake, uncovered, at 400 degrees for 15 to 20 minutes, until biscuits are golden and chicken mixture is hot and bubbly. Makes 6 servings.

Add authentic south-of-the-border flavor to Mexican dishes with quesadilla cheese or crumbly queso fresco, now stocked in many supermarkets. Can't find them? Monterey Jack is a good substitute.

Chicken, Pork &
Beef Mains

Quick Spicy Beef Burritos

Donia Wright
Fort Worth, TX

This started out as a rather fattening taco pie recipe. Over the years, my mother and I have tried to make it a little healthier. For a milder flavor, use plain diced tomatoes and just half of the taco seasoning. The burritos may be wrapped and frozen individually, then reheated in the microwave for one to two minutes. Great for quick meals!

1 lb. lean ground beef
1/4 c. onion, chopped
1-1/4 oz. pkg. taco seasoning
  mix
16-oz. can fat-free refried beans
10-oz. can diced tomatoes and
  green chiles

Optional: salt to taste
5 8-inch whole-wheat tortillas
3/4 c. reduced-fat shredded
  Cheddar cheese

In a skillet over medium heat, brown beef with onion. Drain; stir in taco seasoning. Add beans and undrained tomatoes, stirring until well combined. Simmer for 5 minutes, stirring occasionally. Add salt, if desired. Warm tortillas in the microwave, following package directions. To serve, scoop beef mixture onto tortillas; sprinkle with cheese, roll up tortillas and serve. Makes 5 servings.

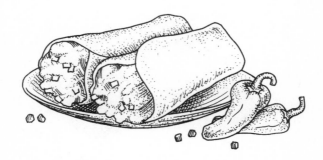

Turn your budding chefs loose in the kitchen! Get a group of kids together to whip up an easy meal like Quick Spicy Beef Burritos. Not only is it a terrific way to teach kids some cooking basics, they'll have a ball cooking with friends.

Harvest Stuffed Pork Chops

Andrea Heyart
Aubrey, TX

These pork chops are a sweet combination of elegance and comfort food...appropriate for both Sunday dinners with the family and autumn dinner parties with friends.

4 thick pork chops
1 c. fresh cranberries
1/4 c. dried cherries
1/3 c. peach preserves
1/4 c. green onions, diced

1/4 t. ground cloves
2 T. honey
salt and pepper to taste
1/4 c. apple butter

Create a pocket in each pork chop by slicing along the side, about 3/4 of the way through. Set aside. Place cranberries in a food processor or blender. Pulse once or twice, until berries are chopped but not puréed. In a bowl, combine cranberries, cherries, preserves, onions, cloves and honey. Stuff cranberry mixture into the pocket in each chop. Season chops on both sides with salt and pepper; arrange in a lightly greased 13"x9" baking pan. Brush the top of each chop evenly with apple butter. Bake, uncovered, at 325 degrees for 40 to 50 minutes, until juices run clear. Makes 4 servings.

If you love fresh cranberries, stock up when they're available and pop unopened bags in the freezer. You'll be able to add their fruity tang to recipes year 'round.

Chicken, Pork & Beef Mains

Rosemary Pork & Mushrooms

Vickie

This simple dish is delicious with ordinary button mushrooms, but for a special dinner I'll use a combination of wild mushrooms...their earthy flavor goes so well with fresh rosemary.

1 lb. pork tenderloin, cut into
    8 slices
1 T. butter
1 c. sliced mushrooms
2 T. onion, finely chopped

1 clove garlic, minced
1 t. fresh rosemary, chopped
1/4 t. celery salt
1 T. sherry or apple juice

Flatten each pork slice to one-inch thick; set aside. Melt butter in a large skillet over medium-high heat. Cook pork slices just until golden, about one minute per side. Remove pork slices to a plate, reserving drippings in skillet. Add remaining ingredients except sherry or apple juice to skillet. Reduce heat to low; cook for 2 minutes, stirring frequently. Stir in sherry or juice. Return pork slices to skillet; spoon mushroom mixture over top. Cover and simmer for 3 to 4 minutes, until pork juices run clear. Serve pork slices topped with mushroom mixture. Makes 4 servings, 2 slices each.

Flattened boneless pork slices cook up quickly and evenly...
works with chicken too! Simply place meat between two pieces
of plastic wrap and gently pound to desired thickness
with a meat mallet or a small skillet.

Kickin' Pasta Sauce

Kristin Stone
Little Elm, TX

*This is my favorite homemade pasta sauce. It's quick, it's easy
and it's got a taste like no other sauce I've ever had!
This recipe is easy to halve and freezes well.*

1 t. olive oil
14-oz. pkg. smoked Italian
   turkey sausage, diced
1 onion, chopped
4 cloves garlic, minced
2 14-1/2 oz. cans Italian-style
   stewed tomatoes, drained
   and juice reserved

2 7-oz. jars roasted red
   peppers, drained
2 t. sugar
1 t. ground cumin
1/2 t. dried oregano
1/2 t. cayenne pepper
1/2 t. salt
1/2 t. red wine vinegar

Heat oil in a large stockpot over medium heat; add sausage, onion
and garlic. Sauté until sausage is golden and onion is tender, about
5 minutes. Meanwhile, combine remaining ingredients in a blender
and blend until puréed, working in batches if necessary. Add tomato
mixture to sausage mixture in stockpot. Reduce heat to low; cover and
simmer to desired consistency, stirring occasionally. Thin sauce with
reserved tomato juice, if desired. Serve sauce ladled over cooked pasta.
Makes 12 servings.

For a tasty change from bread & butter, serve slices of warm
Italian bread with dipping oil. Pour a thin layer of extra-virgin
olive oil into saucers, drizzle with a little balsamic vinegar
and sprinkle with dried oregano. Scrumptious!

Chicken, Pork & Beef Mains

Healthy Spinach Spaghetti

Kelly Serdynski Gray
Weston, WV

While dining out, my boys and I enjoyed a delicious light meal. My husband bet me a dinner out that I could copy the recipe and make it better...he was right! As a busy teacher and mom, I promise this can be made in 15 minutes, hands-down.

8-oz. pkg. whole-wheat
   spaghetti, uncooked
salt to taste
1 onion, chopped
1/2 c. plus 2 T. canola oil,
   divided
2 cloves garlic, pressed
2 10-oz. pkgs. frozen spinach,
   drained and squeezed dry

14-1/2 oz. can diced tomatoes
4 boneless, skinless chicken
   breasts, cooked and cubed
garlic salt, cayenne pepper and
   pepper to taste
1 c. shredded Monterey Jack
   cheese
1/2 c. fresh parsley, chopped
Optional: bacon crumbles

Cook pasta according to package directions, adding salt generously to cooking water. Drain, reserving 3/4 cup of cooking water. Meanwhile, in a skillet over medium heat, sauté onion in 2 tablespoons canola oil until translucent. Stir in garlic, spinach, tomatoes with juice, chicken and reserved cooking water. Add seasonings to taste. Reduce heat to low; heat through for several minutes. Return drained pasta to its cooking pot while still hot. Add remaining oil to pasta; toss to mix. Add spinach mixture to pasta; stir well. Garnish individual servings with cheese, parsley and bacon crumbles, if desired. Makes 8 servings.

Keep some festive paper plates
and napkins tucked away...
they'll set a lighthearted
mood on busy evenings, plus
easy clean-up afterward!

Herbed Apricot Chicken

Anne Alesauskas
Minocqua, WI

I made this recipe for Christmas dinner a few years back.
It is beautiful when it is done, and tasty too. I served it
with a squash risotto.

3 T. extra-virgin olive oil
1/2 onion, sliced
3 lbs. boneless, skinless chicken
    breasts and thighs, cubed
salt and pepper to taste
1/4 c. balsamic vinegar

2 c. chicken broth
20 dried apricots, chopped
5 fresh thyme sprigs
3 T. fresh chives, chopped
zest and juice of 1 lemon

In a large skillet, heat olive oil over medium-high heat. Add onion; sauté for about 5 minutes. Season chicken generously with salt and pepper; add chicken to skillet. Cook, stirring often, until golden on all sides, about 7 to 8 minutes. Add vinegar and stir for 30 seconds. Add broth, apricots and thyme sprigs. Reduce heat to medium-low. Cover and simmer for 10 minutes. Remove from heat. Stir in remaining ingredients; cover and let stand several minutes. Discard thyme sprigs before serving. Makes 6 servings.

Toss sprigs or leaves of garden-fresh herbs like parsley,
chives, mint, dill and basil into a lettuce salad for
a delightfully different taste.

Chicken, Pork & Beef Mains

Chicken Bombay

MaryBeth Summers
Medford, OR

*This simple dish is a bit exotic and has a nice mild flavor.
I will sometimes add some coconut milk to the cooking water
while I'm preparing the rice.*

1/4 c. butter, melted
1 T. curry powder
1 tart apple, peeled, cored and
  chopped

1 onion, chopped
3 lbs. chicken, cut up
2 c. cooked rice

Spread butter in a 13"x9" baking pan; add curry powder and mix
well. Stir in apple and onion. Bake, uncovered, at 400 degrees for
5 minutes. Add chicken to pan, skin-side down. Cover and bake for
25 minutes. Turn chicken over and bake, uncovered, an additional
25 minutes, or until chicken juices run clear. Remove chicken to a
serving platter; stir cooked rice into pan juices and serve. Makes
4 servings.

If you're cooking rice for dinner, why not make some extra?
Frozen in one-cup serving containers, it's easy to reheat later
in the week for a quick lunch or dinner. Especially handy
if you prefer brown rice, which can take a lot longer
to cook than white rice.

Pepper Steak

Cyndi Little
Whitsett, NC

A family favorite go-to meal! Garnish with a sprinkle of crunchy chow mein noodles.

1 lb. lean beef round steak,
   1/2-inch thick
1 T. paprika
2 T. butter
2 cloves garlic, pressed
1-1/2 c. beef broth
1 c. green onions, sliced

2 green peppers, sliced
2 T. cornstarch
1/4 c. cold water
1/4 c. soy sauce
2 tomatoes, cut into
   8 wedges each
3 c. cooked rice

Pound beef to 1/4-inch thickness; cut into 1/4-inch wide strips. Sprinkle beef strips with paprika; let stand for several minutes. In a large skillet over medium-high heat, brown beef in butter. Stir in garlic and broth. Reduce heat to medium-low; cover and simmer for 30 minutes. Stir in onions and green peppers; cover and cook an additional 5 minutes. In a small bowl, blend cornstarch, water and soy sauce; stir into beef mixture. Cook and stir until thickened and clear, about 2 minutes. Add tomatoes and stir gently. Serve beef mixture over cooked rice. Makes 6 servings.

When garden tomatoes aren't in season, try roma tomatoes... they're available year 'round and work well in cooked dishes.

Chicken, Pork & Beef Mains

Katie's Chinese Beef

Katie Cooper
Chubbuck, ID

Every year for my birthday, my mom would let me choose what I wanted her to make for dinner. Year after year it was this delicious dish...so good and it made me feel special!

3 T. sugar
3 T. cornstarch
5 T. soy sauce
1 lb. beef sirloin or round steak,
   thinly sliced into strips
1/4 t. ground ginger
1 clove garlic, chopped
2 T. canola oil, divided

1 green pepper, chopped
1 onion, sliced
2 stalks celery, sliced
2 green onions, chopped
3 tomatoes, chopped
8 mushrooms, sliced
4 c. cooked rice

In a large plastic zipping bag, combine sugar, cornstarch and soy sauce. Add beef to bag; toss to coat well. Close bag; refrigerate 8 hours to overnight, turning bag occasionally. In a skillet over medium-high heat, sauté ginger and garlic in canola oil. Discard garlic. Add vegetables to skillet; cook for 4 minutes, stirring frequently. Remove vegetables to a bowl. Drain beef, discarding marinade; add beef to skillet. Cook beef to desired doneness; drain. Meanwhile, prepare Sauce. Add Sauce and vegetables to beef in skillet; heat through. Serve over cooked rice. Makes 8 servings.

Sauce:

1 c. water
1 cube chicken bouillon
1 T. cornstarch

1 T. sugar
1 T. soy sauce
1 t. salt

In a saucepan over medium heat, cook and stir all ingredients until thickened and dissolved.

To remove an onion smell from your hands, simply rub
your hands with a stainless steel spoon while
holding them under cold running water.

Skillet Apples & Pork Chops

Devi McDonald
Visalia, CA

*Juicy pan-seared pork chops are paired with sautéed apples
and onion...very satisfying. Nothing will make your home
smell more delicious than this dish!*

6 bone-in pork chops
salt and pepper to taste
1/4 c. butter, divided
3 to 4 Granny Smith apples,
   cored and thinly sliced

1 onion, thinly sliced
1/2 t. fresh thyme, chopped
1 c. lager-style beer or
   apple cider

Season pork chops with salt and pepper. Melt half of butter in a skillet
over medium-high heat. Add pork chops to skillet; cook for 5 minutes.
Turn chops over and cook for another 4 minutes, or until juices run
clear. Drain; remove chops to a plate. Reduce heat to medium; add
remaining butter, apples, onion and thyme to skillet. Cook for about
6 minutes, stirring occasionally; add beer or cider. Cook an additional
15 minutes, or until liquid has reduced and thickened. Return chops to
skillet; cover with apple mixture. Cook for 5 minutes. Serve chops
topped with apple mixture. Makes 6 servings.

Here's an easy way to core apples, pears and peaches...slice fruit
in half, then use a melon baller to scoop out the core.

Chicken, Pork & Beef Mains

Cilantro Chicken Skillet

Gail Blain Prather
Stockton, KS

*This recipe is a winner for two reasons...I can use
my favorite cast-iron skillet, and it's budget-friendly.
Perfect for weeknights when we're so busy!*

1 c. long-cooking rice, uncooked
3 T. butter, divided
1 lb. boneless, skinless chicken
   breasts, cubed
1 T. fresh cilantro, chopped
1 T. garlic, finely minced

1 c. onion, chopped
15-oz. can red beans, drained
   and rinsed
Optional: additional chopped
   cilantro
Garnish: hot pepper sauce

Cook rice according to package directions; keep warm. Meanwhile,
in a large skillet over medium-high heat, melt 2 tablespoons butter
until sizzling. Add chicken, cilantro and garlic. Cook, stirring
occasionally, until chicken is no longer pink, about 10 minutes.
Remove chicken from skillet; keep warm. Melt remaining butter in
same skillet; add onion. Cook, stirring occasionally, until onion is
softened, about 4 minutes. Stir in beans and rice. Continue cooking,
stirring occasionally, until heated through. To serve, spoon rice
mixture onto a serving platter; top with chicken. Garnish with
additional cilantro, if desired; serve with hot sauce. Makes 4 servings.

Post a notepad on the fridge to make a note whenever
a kitchen staple is used up...you'll never run out of
that one item you need for dinner.

Chicken Pesto Primo

Tara Horton
Delaware, OH

One summer I grew basil in my garden and froze batches of homemade pesto in ice cube trays. I made up this recipe to use that yummy pesto. When asparagus isn't in season, I'll toss in some broccoli flowerets...it's just as tasty!

8-oz. pkg. rotini pasta, cooked
2 c. cooked chicken, cubed
1 c. asparagus, steamed and cut
    into 1-inch pieces

2 T. basil pesto sauce
1/4 to 1/2 c. chicken broth

Cook pasta according to package directions; drain. In a skillet over medium heat, combine chicken, asparagus, pesto, cooked pasta and 1/4 cup chicken broth. Cook and stir until heated through, adding more broth as needed. Makes 4 servings.

Keep mini pots of your favorite fresh herbs like oregano, chives, parsley and basil on a sunny kitchen windowsill... they'll be right at your fingertips for adding flavor to any dish!

Fish & Vegetable

Mains

Captain's Favorite Tilapia

Diana Migliaccio
Clifton, NJ

*I like to serve rice pilaf and spinach salad
alongside this flavorful fish dish.*

1/4 c. olive oil
1 sweet onion, thinly sliced
1 lb. tilapia fillets
12 Kalamata olives, chopped
8 cloves garlic, chopped

1/4 c. fresh basil, chopped,
   or 1 T. dried basil
2 tomatoes, thinly sliced
salt and pepper to taste
Optional: lemon wedges

Heat olive oil in an oven-proof skillet over medium heat. Sauté onion slices for 3 minutes per side, or until translucent. Arrange fish over onion; sprinkle with olives, garlic and basil. Place tomato slices on top. Add salt and pepper to taste. Remove skillet to center oven rack. Bake, uncovered, at 375 degrees for 12 to 15 minutes, until fish flakes easily with a fork. Garnish with lemon wedges, if desired. Makes 4 servings.

Fish for dinner? Here are a few pointers. At the seafood counter, check for a mild (never fishy!) ocean aroma and fish displayed on clean, well-drained ice. Packages of flash-frozen fish in the store's freezer should be free of frost and ice crystals. Lastly, tuck an ice cooler in the car, to help you keep the day's catch fresh on the way home.

Fish &
Vegetable Mains

Garden-Style Spaghetti

Elizabeth Mullett
Wilmington, MA

This flavorful dish can't be beat when the tomatoes are ripe and the herbs are fresh. We also enjoy this simple tomato and herb mixture spooned onto hamburgers...even bruschetta-style on grilled Italian bread. What a yummy way to use up very ripe tomatoes!

16-oz. pkg. whole-wheat
   spaghetti, uncooked
2 lbs. ripe tomatoes, chopped
3 T. fresh basil, chopped
1 T. fresh rosemary, chopped

1 T. fresh thyme, chopped
1 T. fresh marjoram, chopped
1/2 c. olive oil
6 T. grated Parmesan cheese

Cook pasta according to package directions; drain. Meanwhile, place tomatoes and herbs in a large heat-proof serving bowl; set aside. Heat olive oil in a small saucepan over low heat until very hot. Carefully pour hot oil over tomato mixture; mix well. Add cooked pasta to tomato mixture and stir gently. Serve topped with grated cheese. Makes 6 servings.

Aged Parmesan cheese is most flavorful when it's freshly grated. A chunk of Parmesan will stay fresh in the fridge for several weeks if wrapped in a paper towel dampened with cider vinegar and then tucked into a plastic zipping bag.

Spaghetti with Fresh Tomatoes & Cheddar

Mary Ouellette
New Cumberland, PA

I used to make this dish often when my kids were little, using tomatoes from our garden. They always gobbled it up! For the best flavor, keep the tomatoes at room temperature.

16-oz. pkg. whole-wheat
   spaghetti, uncooked
2 T. olive oil
1 to 2 cloves garlic, finely
   chopped
2 T. butter, sliced
2 lbs. tomatoes, chopped

1/2 c. fresh parsley, chopped
1/4 c. green onion, thinly sliced
1/2 t. salt
1/2 t. pepper
1-1/2 c. shredded sharp
   Cheddar cheese

Cook pasta according to package directions; drain. Meanwhile, heat oil in a small skillet over low heat. Add garlic; sauté just until softened, about 2 minutes. Add butter; stir to melt and remove from heat. Transfer hot pasta to a large heat-proof serving bowl. Add oil mixture and remaining ingredients except cheese; toss to combine. Sprinkle with cheese; toss again until cheese starts to melt through the mixture. Serve immediately. Makes 6 servings.

Good to know! Whole-wheat pasta has a much shorter shelf life than regular white pasta. For the best flavor and nutrition, use it within about 3 months of purchase.

Fish & Vegetable Mains

Potatoes, Peas & Pasta

Cathie Canestaro
Horseheads, NY

*My mother made this simple dish often for meatless meals
and to stretch her grocery allowance. I always loved it
and so do my children.*

1 T. olive oil
6-oz. can tomato paste
4 potatoes, peeled and diced
1-1/4 c. small shell pasta,
   uncooked

salt and pepper to taste
14-1/2 oz. can peas, drained

Heat olive oil in a large saucepan over medium heat. Add tomato
paste; stir well. Add potatoes; stir to coat. Add enough water to cover
potatoes. Cover pan and cook until potatoes are partially cooked, about
10 minutes. Stir in pasta and season with salt; add water as needed to
cover pasta by 1/2 inch. Cook until pasta is tender and water is
absorbed, 8 to 10 minutes. Add pepper and more salt, if needed.
Stir in peas; heat through. Makes 6 servings.

Welcome a new daughter-in-law to the family with this wedding
or shower gift. Gather favorite family recipes in a book for her
and include all the stories that go along with them.

Baked Halibut Fillets

Mary Morris
Uvalda, GA

My husband's cousin has a charter fishing boat in Homer, Alaska, and he sent us some flash-frozen halibut fillets. My mother-in-law and I had never tasted halibut before, so we gave it a try. We loved it so much that we eat halibut quite often now!

3 eggs
1/2 c. milk
4 c. seasoned dry bread crumbs
1 lb. halibut fillets, cut into
    fingers

garlic powder, seasoned salt
    and pepper to taste
3/4 c. butter, sliced

Cover a baking sheet with aluminum foil; spray with non-stick vegetable spray and set aside. In a shallow bowl, whisk together eggs and milk. Place bread crumbs in a separate bowl. Season fish as desired. Place fish in egg mixture; allow to become completely saturated. Dredge fish in bread crumbs, coating completely. Arrange fish on baking sheet; place slices of butter on and between fish. Bake, uncovered, at 350 degrees for 10 minutes. Turn fish over; bake an additional 10 minutes, or until fish flakes easily with a fork. Makes 4 servings.

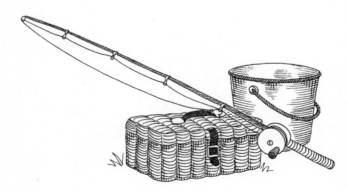

Here's a handy tip to make frozen fish taste fresh and mild...
just place the frozen fillets in a shallow dish, cover with
milk and thaw in the refrigerator overnight.

Fish & Vegetable Mains

Pasta con Broccoli

Lisa Payne
Saint Louis, MO

I love this recipe...it tastes amazing and can be prepared in about 30 minutes! I made some adjustments to cut the fat, and my family can't even tell the difference. Sometimes I stir in some diced grilled chicken to make it heartier.

8-oz. pkg. medium shell pasta,
    uncooked
1/4 c. butter, sliced
1 c. regular half-and-half
1 c. fat-free half-and-half
1/4 c. tomato sauce
1 t. garlic powder
12-oz. pkg. frozen broccoli
    flowerets in steamer bag
1 t. salt
pepper to taste
1/2 c. grated Parmesan cheese

Cook pasta according to package directions for half the time given, about 5 minutes. Drain; return to cooking pot. Stir in butter, half-and-half, tomato sauce and garlic powder; bring to a boil. Meanwhile, microwave broccoli according to package directions; drain. When pasta is just tender, stir in broccoli, salt and pepper. Remove from heat; stir in Parmesan cheese. Makes 4 servings.

Decorate a reusable shopping bag for toting home groceries...
it's so easy, you'll want to make several. Pick up a plain canvas
tote bag from a craft store and attach a big square of pretty fabric
to each side with simple stitching or fabric glue.

Greek Pita Pizzas

Lynda McCormick
Burkburnett, TX

These are my healthy go-to summer pizzas. Kids and adults love them! For a crisper crust, spritz pitas with olive oil spray and sprinkle with coarse salt, then broil for one to 2 minutes before adding the toppings.

10-oz. pkg. frozen chopped
　　spinach, thawed and
　　well drained
4 green onions, chopped
chopped fresh dill to taste
garlic salt and pepper to taste
4 fat-free whole-wheat pita
　　rounds, split

4 roma tomatoes, sliced
　　1/2-inch thick
1/2 c. crumbled feta cheese
　　with basil & tomato
dried oregano or Greek
　　seasoning to taste

Mix spinach, onions and dill in a small bowl. Season with garlic salt and pepper; set aside. Place pita rounds on ungreased baking sheets. Arrange tomato slices among pitas. Spread spinach mixture evenly over tomatoes; spread cheese over tomatoes. Sprinkle with desired seasoning. Bake at 450 degrees for 10 to 15 minutes, until crisp. Cut into wedges. Makes 8 servings.

Shake up a fat-free fresh vinaigrette for salad greens. Fill a cruet bottle with 1/2 cup herb-flavored vinegar, 2 tablespoons water, one tablespoon Dijon mustard, 2 teaspoons Worcestershire sauce, 4 teaspoons sugar or sweetener, 2 pressed garlic cloves and a dash of pepper...shake and enjoy!

Fish & Vegetable Mains

Zucchini-Crust Pizza

Lorinda Herrell
Connersville, IN

My neighbor Joni, who's a registered nurse, shared this recipe with me, as I am diabetic and also a gardener with tons of zucchini. It's a tasty low-carb recipe that's a terrific way to use up zucchini. I tweaked it a little to make it more my own. These crusts freeze very well too. Enjoy!

2 c. zucchini, shredded
   and packed
2 eggs, beaten
1/3 c. whole-wheat flour
1/2 c. shredded mozzarella
   cheese

1/2 c. shredded pizza-blend
   cheese
1 T. olive oil
1 T. fresh basil, chopped
Garnish: favorite pizza toppings

In a strainer, press zucchini to remove as much liquid as possible. Combine zucchini and remaining ingredients except garnish in a bowl; stir well. Spread in a parchment paper-lined 12" round pizza pan. Smooth out mixture to cover pan. Bake at 375 degrees for 35 minutes, or until set. Top with desired toppings; return to oven until heated through. Cut into wedges to serve. Makes 6 servings.

Let the kids lend a hand in the kitchen! Preschoolers can wash veggies, fold napkins and set the table. Older children can measure, shred, chop, stir and maybe even help with meal planning and grocery shopping.

Brown Butter Gnocchi & Spinach

Chad Rutan
Gooseberry Patch

A super-simple dish to toss together on a weeknight. Take a few basic ingredients plus just a little time and you've got yourself a great-tasting dish!

16-oz. pkg. refrigerated gnocchi
    pasta, uncooked
2 T. butter
2 T. pine nuts
2 cloves garlic, minced

1/2 lb. fresh spinach, torn
1/4 t. salt
1/4 t. pepper
1/4 c. grated Parmesan cheese

Cook pasta according to package directions; drain. Meanwhile, melt butter in a large skillet over medium heat. Add pine nuts to skillet. Cook, stirring constantly, for 3 minutes, or until butter and nuts are golden. Add garlic to skillet; cook for one minute. Add pasta and spinach. Cook, stirring constantly, for one minute, or until spinach wilts. Sprinkle with salt and pepper; stir in cheese. Makes 4 servings.

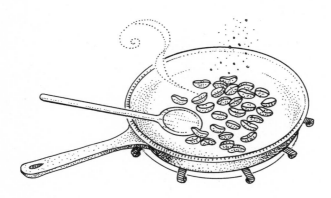

Toasting nuts is so easy. Place them in a dry skillet over medium heat. Stir occasionally until lightly golden, about 3 minutes. Cool before adding to your recipe.

Fish & Vegetable Mains

Fresh Veggies & Angel Hair

Kelli Venable
Ostrander, OH

*My mom & I love this yummy summertime meal...just add
a slice or two of garlic bread and enjoy!*

7-oz. pkg. angel hair pasta,
   uncooked
1 T. olive oil
2 zucchini, peeled if desired
   and diced

2 yellow squash, diced
1 c. sliced mushrooms
1/2 c. onion, chopped
salt and pepper to taste

Divide pasta in half; reserve one-half for another recipe. Cook
remaining pasta according to package directions; drain. Meanwhile,
heat oil in a skillet over medium heat. Add zucchini, yellow squash,
mushrooms and onion to skillet; cook until crisp-tender. Season with
salt and pepper; ladle sauce over pasta. Makes 2 servings.

Be sure to wash fresh produce well under cold water. Firm fruits
and vegetables like apples and potatoes can be scrubbed with a
veggie brush, while tender varieties like tomatoes and pears can
simply be rinsed well. There's no need to use soap, but add
a bit of vinegar or baking soda to the rinse water if you like.

Homemade Fish Sticks

Shelley Turner
Boise, ID

*My kids love these yummy fish sticks! I serve them in diner-style
baskets with French fries and some celery sticks or baby carrots.
No forks needed...dinner doesn't need to be serious!*

2 lbs. cod fillets
2 eggs
2 T. water
salt and pepper to taste
1-1/2 c. seasoned dry bread
    crumbs

3 T. grated Parmesan cheese
1/4 c. olive oil
1/2 c. tartar sauce
Garnish: lemon wedges

Cut fish into 4-inch by 2-inch strips; set aside. In a shallow dish,
beat together egg, water and seasonings. In a separate dish, mix bread
crumbs and cheese. Dip fish into egg mixture; coat with bread crumb
mixture and set aside. Heat olive oil in a skillet over medium-high
heat. Working in batches, add fish to skillet and cook until flaky and
golden, about 3 minutes per side. Drain fish sticks on paper towels.
Serve with tartar sauce and lemon wedges. Makes 8 servings.

Mix up a quick homemade tartar sauce for your next fish dinner!
Combine 1/2 cup mayonnaise, 2 tablespoons sweet pickle relish
and one tablespoon lemon juice. Chill until serving time.

Fish &
Vegetable Mains

Sisters' Baked Harvest Vegetables
Stacy Lane
Laurel, DE

When my sister Michelle and I were in college, we were vegetarians, and this is the dish we made every year when we came home for Thanksgiving. We're grown up now, but we still make this dish for our families! It's so easy and delicious.

4 potatoes, or 2 potatoes and
   2 turnips, peeled and cubed
1 bunch broccoli, cut into bite-
   size flowerets
2 c. green beans, trimmed
3 carrots, peeled and sliced into
   1/4-inch thick rounds

1 zucchini, sliced into 1/4-inch
   thick rounds
1 yellow squash, sliced into
   1/4-inch thick rounds
1/2 c. olive oil
1.35-oz. pkg. onion soup mix

Combine all vegetables in a lightly greased 13"x9" baking pan. Drizzle with olive oil and toss to coat. Sprinkle with soup mix and toss again. Bake, uncovered, at 350 degrees for about 45 minutes, until all vegetables are tender. Makes 8 servings.

Stuffed tomatoes are delicious and fun to eat! Scoop out the pulp and prebake the shells at 350 degrees for 10 minutes. Fill with your favorite seasoned rice or dressing and bake for an additional 10 minutes, until hot. Top with shredded cheese, if you like.

Parmesan Zucchini & Spaghetti *Jennifer Brandes Leroy, NY*

We grew so much zucchini in our garden that I had to come up with some creative recipes. Here's one I tried...my family loved it!

16-oz. pkg. spaghetti, uncooked
2 zucchini, cubed
2 yellow squash, cubed
1/2 c. onion, diced
1 clove garlic, minced

2 T. butter
1/2 c. milk
1/2 c. grated Parmesan cheese
pepper to taste

Cook spaghetti according to package directions; drain. Meanwhile, in a skillet over medium heat, sauté zucchini, squash, onion and garlic in butter until tender. Add milk and cheese to mixture in skillet; whisk until thickened into a sauce. Season with pepper. Serve zucchini mixture over spaghetti. Makes 6 servings.

Keep a few packages of frozen cheese ravioli, tortellini or pierogies tucked in the freezer for easy meal-making anytime. Quickly cooked and topped with your favorite sauce, they're terrific as either a side dish or a meatless main.

Fish & Vegetable Mains

Shrimp & Mushroom Fettuccine

Dani Simmers
Kendallville, IN

An excellent dish for company because it's oh-so-good and a little different. Serve with a fresh green salad, a basket of warm Italian bread and a big shaker of shredded Parmesan cheese.

12-oz. pkg. garlic & herb
   fettuccine pasta, uncooked
2 T. olive oil
1 lb. cooked medium shrimp
1 lb. sliced mushrooms

2 T. garlic, minced
10-oz. pkg. fresh spinach,
   thinly sliced
2 c. tomato sauce
2 T. chicken soup base

Cook pasta according to package directions; drain. Meanwhile, heat olive oil in a large skillet over medium heat. Sauté shrimp, mushrooms, garlic and spinach for several minutes, until mushrooms are tender and spinach is wilted. Remove mixture to a bowl with a slotted spoon, reserving drippings in skillet. Add tomato sauce and soup base to drippings. Stir well and bring to a boil. Return shrimp mixture to skillet and heat through; add cooked pasta and toss together. Makes 6 servings.

Try using chicken broth instead of oil to sauté or stir-fry. When opening a can of broth, remove any fat from surface, use what you need, and pour the extra into ice cube trays and freeze. The next time you need a little broth, pop out a cube and place it in your frying pan.

Black Beans & Saffron Rice

Sandy Barnhart
Sapulpa, OK

This is a really good vegetarian recipe...it's easy to fix and takes less than 30 minutes to make. We like to dig in using scoop-type tortilla chips or blue corn chips instead of a spoon. I'm sure you'll make this one of your regular meals too!

2 5-oz. pkgs. saffron yellow
   rice, uncooked
2 T. butter
3/4 c. onion, chopped
3 stalks celery, chopped

1 T. garlic, minced
2 16-oz. cans black beans
1 t. ground cumin
Optional: garlic powder to taste
3/4 c. pico de gallo or salsa

Cook rice according to package directions. Meanwhile, in a separate saucepan over medium heat, melt butter; add onion, celery and garlic. Sauté for 3 to 4 minutes, just until crisp-tender. Stir in beans with liquid and cumin. Reduce heat to medium-low; simmer for 10 to 15 minutes. Season with more cumin or garlic powder, if desired. To serve, divide rice into individual bowls; top with bean mixture. Garnish with pico de gallo or salsa. Makes 6 servings.

Whip up a bowl of fresh pico de gallo to go with your next Mexican meal. Combine diced tomatoes with a little onion and jalapeño pepper. Add lime juice and garlic salt to taste and serve immediately.

Fish & Vegetable Mains

Vegetarian Mexican Pie

Sonya Labbe
West Hollywood, CA

When we moved to Los Angeles, I started searching for Mexican dishes that my family would love. This recipe is one of them. It's easy to make, yet so much better than fast food.

12 6-inch corn tortillas
1 c. black beans, drained
   and rinsed
1 c. red kidney beans, drained
   and rinsed

4-oz. can chopped green chiles
1-1/2 c. green or red salsa
1 c. sour cream
2 c. shredded Monterey Jack
   cheese

Layer 4 tortillas in a lightly greased 8"x8" baking pan, overlapping slightly. Top tortillas with 1/2 cup black beans, 1/2 cup kidney beans, 1/4 cup chiles, 1/2 cup salsa, 1/3 cup sour cream and 2/3 cup cheese. Add 4 more tortillas; repeat layering. Top with remaining tortillas, salsa, sour cream and cheese. Bake, uncovered, at 375 degrees, until bubbly and golden, 30 to 40 minutes. Makes 4 servings.

Reduced-fat dairy products like milk, sour cream, cream cheese and shredded cheese can be just as tasty. They're an easy substitute for their full-fat counterparts in recipes.

Vegetable Quinoa Patties

Evelyn Moriarty
Philadelphia, PA

This recipe is my own, adapted from one I found online and tweaked. It has become a family favorite, especially in summertime when fresh-picked veggies are available.

3 eggs
1/2 c. shredded Cheddar or
   mozzarella cheese
1/2 c. cottage cheese
1/4 c. whole-wheat flour
1 carrot, peeled and grated
1 zucchini, grated
3 T. green, red or yellow pepper,
   grated

3 green onions, finely chopped
1/2 t. ground cumin
1/4 t. garlic powder
1/8 t. salt
1/4 t. pepper
2 c. cooked quinoa
1 T. olive oil

Beat eggs in a large bowl; stir in cheeses and flour, blending well. Mix in vegetables. Combine seasonings; sprinkle over vegetable mixture and mix well. Add cooked quinoa; stir together well. Heat olive oil in a skillet over medium heat. With a small ladle, drop mixture into skillet, making 4 patties. Flatten lightly with ladle to about 1/4-inch thick. Fry patties for 4 to 5 minutes per side, until golden. Serve with Dilled Yogurt Dressing. Makes 4 servings.

Dilled Yogurt Dressing:

1/2 c. plain Greek yogurt
1 cucumber, peeled and diced

3 sprigs fresh dill, snipped,
   or 1/2 t. dill weed

Stir together all ingredients in a small bowl.

Fish &
Vegetable Mains

Lynda's Salmon Burgers

Lynda McCormick
Burkburnett, TX

Healthy burgers everyone will enjoy! These burgers are just as good without the bread...serve as a salad over fresh spinach with cucumber sauce, sliced avocados, tomatoes and red onion.

1 lb. salmon fillet, skin removed
   and chopped
1/2 c. red onion, finely chopped
1/4 c. fresh basil, thinly sliced
1/4 t. salt
1/4 t. pepper

1 egg white
1 T. sriracha hot chili sauce
Optional: 1/4 c. panko bread
   crumbs
8 slices focaccia bread, toasted

In a large bowl, combine salmon, onion, basil and seasonings; mix gently. In a small bowl, whisk together egg white and chili sauce. Add to salmon mixture and stir well to combine. If mixture is too soft, stir in bread crumbs. Form mixture into 4 patties, 1/2-inch thick. Heat a large non-stick skillet over medium-high heat. Coat pan with non-stick vegetable spray. Add patties to skillet; cook for about 3 minutes per side. Serve patties sandwich-style on toasted focaccia. Makes 4 servings.

Some like it hot! There are lots of ways to turn up the heat in familiar recipes...hot pepper sauce, creamy horseradish, hot Chinese mustard, Japanese wasabi or sriracha from Thailand. Try 'em all...see what you like best!

Baked Flounder & Tomatoes

Nancie Flynn
Bear Creek Twp., PA

*Delicious and so easy to prepare! Mahi-mahi, snapper or
any whitefish fillets are excellent in this recipe too.*

2 ripe tomatoes, sliced
salt and pepper to taste
chopped fresh dill to taste
1 c. Italian-seasoned dry bread
   crumbs, divided

1-1/2 lbs. flounder fillets
1/4 c. butter, melted
1/4 c. grated Parmesan cheese
paprika to taste

Arrange tomato slices in a lightly greased 13"x9" baking pan. Season
lightly with salt and pepper; sprinkle with dill and 1/2 cup bread
crumbs. Arrange fish fillets over tomatoes; season with additional salt
and pepper. Top with remaining bread crumbs and additional dill.
Drizzle with melted butter; sprinkle with Parmesan cheese and paprika.
Bake, uncovered, at 425 degrees for 10 to 15 minutes, just until fish
flakes easily with a fork. Makes 6 servings.

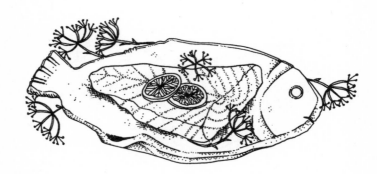

Need a quick, tasty side? Stir sautéed diced mushrooms,
onion, green pepper or celery into prepared wild rice mix
for a homemade touch.

Fish & Vegetable Mains

Summer Squash Pie

Kelly Patrick
Ashburn, VA

My mother and I have used this recipe every summer when summer squash is abundant. It's a very simple, one-bowl recipe that takes literally five minutes to toss together...it's never failed us! Feel free to try different cheeses or add your favorite chopped veggies.

3 c. yellow squash, peeled
   and diced
1/2 c. onion, chopped
4 eggs, beaten
1/3 c. canola oil

1 c. biscuit baking mix
1/2 c. shredded mozzarella
   cheese
salt and pepper to taste

Mix all ingredients in a bowl. Pat into a 9" pie plate lightly coated with non-stick vegetable spray. Bake at 350 degrees for 50 minutes to one hour, until set. Let stand for 10 minutes; slice into wedges. Serve warm or cold. Makes 6 to 8 servings.

Cooked vegetables that your kids refuse to eat may taste better to them crunchy and raw. Serve cut-up fresh veggies or apples with small cups of creamy yogurt, peanut butter or hummus for dunking...problem solved!

Pesto Polenta Lasagna

Lori Rosenberg
University Heights, OH

Nowadays we all have vegetarians at our holiday tables...
this savory dish is a crowd-pleaser for meat-eaters too!

18-oz. tube polenta, sliced
   1/4-inch thick and divided
1/4 c. basil pesto sauce, divided

1-1/4 c. marinara sauce, divided
1 c. shredded mozzarella cheese
1/4 c. pine nuts

In a greased 11"x7" baking pan, arrange half of polenta slices in a single layer. Spread half of pesto over polenta; spoon half of marinara sauce over. Repeat layering, ending with marinara sauce. Bake, uncovered, at 375 degrees for 25 minutes. Remove from oven; top with cheese and pine nuts. Place pan under a preheated broiler; broil until cheese is melted and nuts are toasted. Makes 8 servings.

Made of cornmeal, ready-to-use polenta is a tasty change from rice and potatoes. Try it topped with spaghetti sauce and cheeses, or simply sautéed with butter or olive oil until golden.

Fish & Vegetable Mains

Savory Barley-Mushroom Bake

Dale Duncan
Waterloo, IA

A terrific meatless main or side dish that takes just minutes to put together. If time is short, bake it the night before and rewarm at dinnertime.

1/4 c. butter
1 onion, diced
1 c. mushrooms, chopped
1 c. pearled barley, uncooked
1/2 c. pine nuts or slivered
  almonds

2 green onions, thinly sliced
1/2 c. fresh parsley, chopped
1/4 t. salt
1/8 t. pepper
2 14-1/2 oz. cans vegetable
  or chicken broth

Melt butter in a skillet over medium-high heat. Stir in onion, mushrooms, uncooked barley and nuts. Cook and stir until barley is lightly golden, about 4 to 5 minutes. Stir in green onions and parsley. Season with salt and pepper. Spoon mixture into a lightly greased 2-quart casserole dish; stir in broth. Cover and bake at 350 degrees for one hour and 15 minutes, or until barley is tender and broth has been absorbed. Makes 6 servings.

A permanent marker makes it a snap to keep food cans and boxes rotated in the pantry. Just write the purchase date on each item as groceries are unpacked.

Easy Poached Salmon

JoAnn

An elegant dinner for guests...or treat your family! I like to serve tender roasted asparagus with this salmon.

1 c. water
1/2 c. white wine or vegetable
  broth
1/2 c. onion, sliced

2 sprigs fresh parsley, snipped
5 peppercorns
1/4 t. salt
1 lb. salmon fillets

In a one-quart microwave-safe dish, combine all ingredients except fish; stir well. Cover with plastic wrap. Microwave on high for 2 to 3 minutes, until mixture boils. Discard peppercorns, if desired. Place fish in a separate microwave-safe dish. Pour mixture over fish. Cover and microwave on medium-high for 5 to 6 minutes, until fish flakes easily with a fork. Carefully remove fish to a serving plate. Serve immediately, or chill and serve cold. Serve with Creamy Dijon Sauce. Makes 4 servings.

Creamy Dijon Sauce:

1/2 c. sour cream
1 T. Dijon mustard

1 T. lemon juice
2 t. fresh dill, chopped

Combine all ingredients; mix well and chill before serving.

Roasted cherry tomatoes make a delightful garnish. Place tomatoes (still on the stem, if you like) in a small casserole dish and drizzle with olive oil. Bake at 450 degrees for 15 minutes, or until soft and slightly wrinkled. Serve warm or chilled.

Fish & Vegetable Mains

Sautéed Tilapia in Lemony Butter Sauce

Shirin Blackwell
Garden Ridge, TX

Quick & easy! My daughter loves this nutritious dish with a side of steamed green beans and smashed new potatoes.

1/4 c. all-purpose flour
salt and pepper to taste
1/2 lb. tilapia fillets

2 T. olive oil
4 T. butter, divided
juice of 1 lemon

Combine flour, salt and pepper in a shallow dish. Dredge fish in flour mixture; set aside. Heat olive oil and 2 tablespoons butter in a skillet over medium-high heat. Sauté fish in oil mixture for 3 minutes per side. Remove fish to a plate; wipe out skillet with a paper towel. Reduce heat to low; melt remaining butter in skillet. Add lemon juice; cook and stir for about one minute. Return fish to skillet and warm through. To serve, spoon sauce from skillet over fish. Makes 2 servings.

Make a simple, satisfying side in a jiffy with a package of thin spaghetti. Toss cooked pasta with a little butter and grated Parmesan cheese, or try chopped tomato and a drizzle of olive oil...that's all it takes!

Pinto Bean Dinner

Moriah Clark
Butler, OH

We love all kinds of Mexican food! We have friends who are vegetarian, and we love to serve this dish when they visit.

9-oz. pkg. tortilla chips, crushed
2 30-oz. cans pinto beans,
    drained and rinsed
15-oz. corn, drained
14-1/2 oz. can petite diced
    tomatoes, drained
8-oz. can tomato sauce

1-1/4 oz. pkg. taco seasoning
    mix, or more to taste
2 c. shredded Cheddar cheese
Garnish: sour cream, salsa,
    shredded lettuce,
    sliced black olives

Sprinkle crushed tortilla chips into a greased 13"x9" baking pan; set aside. In a large bowl, combine beans, corn, tomatoes, tomato sauce and taco seasoning; mix well. Spoon mixture over chips; sprinkle with cheese. Bake, uncovered, at 350 degrees for 20 to 25 minutes, until bubbly and heated through. Serve with desired toppings. Makes 8 servings.

A speedy side that goes with any south-of-the-border meal!
Stir some salsa and shredded cheese into hot cooked rice. Cover
and let stand a few minutes until the cheese melts.

Fish & Vegetable Mains

Monastery Lentils

Diane Fliss
Arvada, CO

A friend gave me this meatless recipe many years ago. Serve it with a crisp tossed salad and warm cornbread for a wonderful supper.

1 c. dried lentils, uncooked
3 c. water
1 bay leaf
2 to 4 T. olive oil
1 onion, chopped
2 cloves garlic, minced

1 carrot, peeled and grated
1 c. tomatoes, diced
2 T. fresh parsley, snipped
1 t. dried basil
1 t. salt

Combine lentils, water and bay leaf in a large saucepan; bring to a boil over medium-high heat. Reduce heat to low; cover and simmer for time directed on package, until lentils are tender. Meanwhile, heat olive oil in a skillet over medium heat. Add onion, garlic and carrot to skillet; sauté until onion is translucent, about 5 minutes. Stir onion mixture into lentil mixture; add remaining ingredients. Cover and cook over low heat for 20 minutes. Discard bay leaf before serving. Makes 5 servings.

Dried lentils come in green, black, yellow and the familiar brown color. Each type cooks a little differently, so be sure to check the package directions for the right cooking time.

Very Veggie Mac & Cheese

Stefanie Schmidt
Las Vegas, NV

My mom used to sneak our vegetables into this dish. I loved the taste, and she loved that it was healthy and delicious. This is still my favorite comfort food dish because it tastes so good and reminds me of Mom.

8-oz. pkg. elbow macaroni, uncooked
1 c. carrots, peeled and sliced
1 c. broccoli, chopped
1 c. cauliflower, chopped
1-1/4 c. fat-free milk
2 T. cornstarch
2 T. extra-virgin olive oil

1 onion, chopped
4 cloves garlic, minced
1/2 c. reduced-fat shredded Monterey Jack cheese
1/2 c. reduced-fat shredded Cheddar cheese
1/4 c. reduced-fat cream cheese

Prepare macaroni according to package directions; add vegetables to cooking water during the last 5 minutes of cooking time. Drain; place in a serving bowl. Meanwhile, whisk together milk and cornstarch in a bowl; set aside. Heat oil in a large saucepan over medium heat. Add onion and garlic; cook, stirring frequently, for about 5 minutes. Add milk mixture to onion mixture; bring to a boil, stirring constantly. Reduce heat to low; add cheeses. Cook and stir until cheeses are melted; pour over macaroni mixture. Toss until well combined. Makes 8 servings.

Part of the secret of success in life is to eat what you like and let the food fight it out inside.
— Mark Twain

Fish & Vegetable Mains

Tortellini with Artichokes & Roasted Peppers

Regina Wickline
Pebble Beach, CA

We love this fresh-tasting dish that can be made year 'round from pantry items.

8-oz. pkg. cheese tortellini, uncooked
2 6-oz. jars marinated artichoke hearts, drained
2 T. butter
2 T. olive oil

12-oz. jar roasted red peppers, drained and chopped
1/4 c. fresh basil, chopped, or 1 T. dried basil
salt and pepper to taste

Prepare tortellini according to package directions. Drain, reserving 1/4 cup cooking liquid, and return tortellini to pan. Meanwhile, melt butter and oil in a skillet over medium-high heat. Add artichokes and red peppers. Cook for 5 minutes, stirring often. Add artichoke mixture, reserved cooking liquid and basil to tortellini. Season with salt and pepper; toss to combine. Makes 4 servings.

For hearty salads in a snap, keep unopened cans and jars of diced tomatoes, black olives, garbanzo beans and marinated artichokes in the fridge. They'll be chilled and ready to toss with fresh greens or cooked pasta at a moment's notice.

Kaletti Stir-Fry

Marilyn Moseley
Oldtown, ID

One evening I needed a quick healthy dinner. I had lots of veggies in the refrigerator, so I cooked up this all-veggie dish. My kids loved it, and it's become a favorite. We call it Kaletti because it's kale and spaghetti squash. Who would guess that healthy veggies could taste so good!

1 spaghetti squash, halved
1 T. sesame oil
3 c. broccoli, chopped
1 sweet potato, peeled and cubed
3 carrots, peeled and sliced
1 onion, diced
1 green pepper, sliced

1 red pepper, sliced
1 jalapeño pepper, seeded and diced
1 lb. kale, torn and stems removed
2 cloves garlic, minced
2 T. soy sauce, or to taste

Place spaghetti squash halves on a 15"x10" jelly-roll pan, cut-side down; add 1/2 inch water to baking sheet. Bake, uncovered, at 350 degrees for 15 to 20 minutes, until tender. Meanwhile, heat sesame oil in a large skillet; add all vegetables except kale and garlic. Cook, stirring frequently, until tender, about 10 minutes. Add kale and garlic; cook and stir until kale is wilted, about 5 minutes. Remove from heat. Using a fork, scrape strands from spaghetti squash into skillet. Mix well; return skillet to low heat and heat through. Stir in soy sauce to taste; serve immediately. Makes 6 servings.

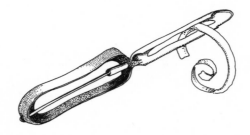

Don't toss out the stalks when preparing fresh broccoli... they're good to eat too. Peel stalks with a potato peeler, then chop or dice and add to salads, stir-fries, salads or soups.

Fish & Vegetable Mains

3-Tomato Penne Pasta

Nancy Girard
Chesapeake, VA

This recipe is a family favorite...it's easy enough for weeknight dinners, yet elegant enough for guests!

12-oz. pkg. penne pasta,
   uncooked
1 t. olive oil
1/2 c. onion, chopped
2 cloves garlic, minced
14-1/2 oz. can diced tomatoes
1/4 c. oil-packed sun-dried
   tomatoes, drained and
   chopped

4 roma tomatoes, chopped
1 t. sugar
1/4 t. salt
1/4 t. pepper
3/4 c. shredded mozzarella
   cheese, or 1/2 c. crumbled
   goat cheese
chopped fresh parsley and
   basil to taste

Cook pasta according to package directions. Drain; return pasta to pan. Meanwhile, heat oil in a large skillet over medium-high heat. Add onion to skillet; sauté until tender, about 4 minutes. Add garlic and sauté for one to 2 minutes, just until golden. Stir in diced tomatoes with juice, sun-dried tomatoes, roma tomatoes and seasonings. Reduce heat to medium-low. Simmer, stirring frequently, for 20 minutes. Add tomato mixture to pasta along with cheese and herbs. Mix lightly and serve. Makes 4 to 6 servings.

To grate or shred a block of cheese easily, place the wrapped cheese in the freezer for 10 to 20 minutes...it will just glide across the grater!

Pasta with Eggplant Sauce

Karen Grafano
Brick, NJ

I love this simple, healthy way to cook eggplant! This dish
can even be served as a dip. If you wish, add 1/2 pound
ground beef, browned along with the onion and garlic.

8-oz. pkg. ziti or rotini pasta,
   uncooked
2 eggplants
4 tomatoes, chopped, or
   14-1/2 oz. can diced
   tomatoes, drained

1 onion, chopped
2 cloves garlic, minced
2 T. olive oil
1 t. dried basil
salt and pepper to taste

Cook pasta according to package directions; drain. Meanwhile,
pierce eggplants several times with a knife; set on a paper towel in a
microwave-safe dish. Microwave, uncovered, for about 12 minutes,
until soft. Slice eggplants open and allow to cool slightly. Scoop out
pulp and place in a bowl, discarding skins. Add tomatoes to eggplant;
set aside. In a small skillet over medium heat, sauté onion and garlic in
olive oil. Add onion mixture and seasonings to eggplant mixture. To
serve, ladle eggplant sauce over pasta. Makes 4 servings.

Eggplants stay fresh just a few days, so it's best to keep them
stored in the crisper of the refrigerator, unwrapped. They'll be
ready for any garden-fresh recipe for about one week.

Fish &
Vegetable Mains

Cheese & Spinach Pie

Amy Hunt
Traphill, NC

Quick, easy and delicious! Your family won't even miss the meat. Pop some garlic bread in the oven alongside your pie, and dinner is ready.

16-oz. container low-fat cottage
    cheese
10-oz. pkg. frozen spinach,
    thawed and well drained
1-1/4 c. shredded part-skim
    mozzarella cheese

1/3 c. grated Parmesan cheese
4 eggs, beaten
1/2 c. red pepper, diced
1/4 c. onion, finely diced
1 t. Italian seasoning

Spray a 9" pie plate with non-stick vegetable spray. In a large bowl, combine all ingredients. Stir until well blended; spoon into pie plate. Bake at 350 degrees for 40 to 45 minutes, until set. Cool slightly; cut into wedges. Makes 8 servings.

Just-picked herbs and creamery butter...yum! Blend one cup butter with 2 tablespoons fresh parsley, 2 teaspoons fresh oregano and one tablespoon minced garlic. Spread over warm rolls, toss with hot noodles or dollop on steamed veggies...delicious.

Shrimp Scampi & Asparagus

Linda Karner
Pisgah Forest, NC

We love fresh asparagus when it comes in season, and I always try to find new ways of using it. This is a recipe I came up with...my husband just loves it!

16-oz. pkg. linguine pasta, uncooked
1 T. salt
2 T. butter
2 T. olive oil
1 lb. asparagus, trimmed and cut into bite-size pieces
2 cloves garlic, minced
2 lbs. medium shrimp, peeled and cleaned

2 T. mixed fresh herbs like basil, thyme, oregano and chives, chopped
2 T. capers, drained
juice of 1/2 lemon
salt and pepper to taste
Optional: 1 T. additional butter and/or olive oil
1/2 c. shredded Parmesan cheese, divided

Cook pasta according to package directions, adding salt to cooking water; drain when pasta is just tender. Meanwhile, in a large skillet over medium heat, melt butter with olive oil. Add asparagus and sauté until partially tender, about 5 minutes. Stir in garlic and shrimp. Cook until shrimp is bright pink, about 5 to 7 minutes. Add herbs, capers and lemon juice; heat through. Season with salt and pepper. Add pasta to mixture in skillet; toss well. If desired, stir in additional butter and/or olive oil. Add 1/4 cup Parmesan cheese and toss again. Serve garnished with remaining cheese. Makes 6 servings.

Keep frozen shrimp on hand for delicious meals anytime. Thaw overnight in the fridge, or for a quicker way, place the frozen shrimp in a colander and run ice-cold water over them. Avoid thawing shrimp in the microwave, as they will turn mushy.

Healthy

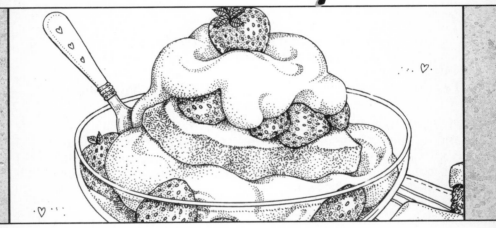

Snacks &
Desserts

Artichoke Frittata

Karen Lee Puchnick
Butler, PA

Yummy and oh-so easy to make! Cut it into larger slices for
a terrific brunch dish. If you're fortunate to have fresh herbs
on hand, use 3/8 teaspoon of each herb.

2 6-oz. jars marinated
   artichokes, drained and
   2 T. marinade reserved
4 eggs, beaten
1 c. ricotta cheese

1 onion, chopped
1/8 t. dried rosemary
1/8 t. dried thyme
1/8 t. dried basil
1/8 t. dried marjoram

Finely chop artichokes; place in a bowl. Add reserved marinade
and remaining ingredients; mix well. Spread mixture into a greased
8"x8" baking pan. Bake at 350 degrees for 30 minutes, or until
set and golden. Cut into one-inch squares; serve warm. Makes
16 servings, 4 pieces each.

A casual appetizer party is perfect for catching up with
family & friends. Everyone is sure to discover new favorites,
so be sure to have each person bring along extra copies
of their recipe to share.

Healthy
Snacks & Desserts

Chickpea & Red
Pepper Dip

Paulette Alexander
Saint George's, Newfoundland

*The first time I made this flavorful recipe, I knew it was a keeper...
everybody loved it! Serve with toasted pita wedges.*

19-oz. can garbanzo beans,
   drained and rinsed
12-oz. jar roasted red peppers,
   drained and sliced
1/2 c. sour cream

1 to 2 cloves garlic, chopped
1/2 t. red pepper flakes
1/4 t. salt
1/4 t. pepper

Combine all ingredients in a food processor or blender. Process until
smooth; transfer to a serving dish. Makes 8 servings, or about 2 cups.

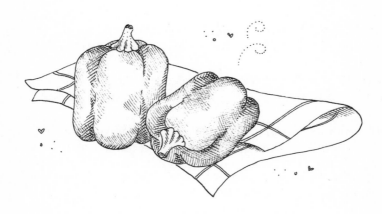

Make your own roasted red peppers! Place whole sweet
peppers on a broiler pan. Broil until blackened on all sides,
turning with tongs. Transfer peppers to a bowl and cover tightly
with plastic wrap. Let stand for about 15 minutes; skins should
peel off easily. Cut into strips and refrigerate for 2 to 3 days,
covering with olive oil if desired.

Traditional Hummus

Louise McGaha
Clinton, TN

I love this recipe...it's just right for a snack or a quick lunch.

2 15-oz. cans garbanzo beans,
   drained and rinsed
1/2 c. warm water
3 T. lime or lemon juice

1 T. tahini sesame seed paste
1-1/2 t. ground cumin
1 T. garlic, minced
1 t. salt

Place all ingredients in a food processor or blender. Process until very smooth, about 4 minutes. If a thinner consistency is desired, add an extra tablespoon or two of water. Transfer to a serving bowl. Makes 8 servings, or about 2 cups.

Perfect Party Pita Chips

Stefanie Schmidt
Las Vegas, NV

I love hosting parties on game days! These chips taste fantastic and go perfectly with hummus, salsa, ranch dip and other dips.

4 6-inch whole-wheat pita
   rounds, split

8 t. olive oil
2 cloves garlic, pressed

Cut each split pita round in half; cut each half into 4 triangles. In a small bowl, combine olive oil and garlic in a small bowl; brush over triangles. Arrange triangles in a single layer on an ungreased baking sheet. Bake at 350 degrees for 8 to 10 minutes, until crisp and golden. Makes 8 servings, about 4 chips each.

A festive container for chips in a jiffy! Simply tie a knot
in each corner of a brightly colored bandanna,
then tuck a bowl into the center.

Healthy
Snacks & Desserts

Avocado Feta Dip

Anne Alesauskas
Minocqua, WI

My family doesn't care for tomatoes but we love red peppers.
So I just substituted them for the tomatoes in this recipe...
it's delicious! Serve with tortilla chips or baguette slices.

2 avocados, halved, pitted
   and diced
1 c. crumbled feta cheese
1 red pepper, diced

1 green onion, thinly sliced
1 T. lemon juice
2 t. dill weed
salt and pepper to taste

Combine all ingredients in a serving bowl; mix until smooth. Makes 12 servings, or about 3 cups.

Fresh, ripe avocados are wonderful in dips and salads.
To determine ripeness, gently press at the pointy end. If it gives,
it's ripe! If it's still a bit firm, place in a paper bag at room
temperature. Store ripe avocados in the refrigerator.

White Bean Hummus

Lisa McGee
Fredericton, New Brunswick

A lower-fat hummus that's made with white beans instead of the usual chickpeas. Change up the seasonings as you like...I've sometimes used fresh rosemary instead of cumin and chili powder. Very tasty with pitas and veggies!

19-oz. can white kidney beans,
   drained and rinsed
1 T. fresh parsley, chopped
1 T. lemon juice
1 T. olive oil

1/4 t. ground cumin
1/4 t. chili powder
1 clove garlic, chopped
salt and pepper to taste

Combine all ingredients in a food processor or blender; process until smooth. Cover and chill for about one hour before serving. Makes 8 servings, or about 2 cups.

Try serving "light" dippers with hearty full-flavored dips and spreads. Bite-size baby vegetables, pita wedges, baked tortilla chips and multi-grain crispbread are all sturdy enough to scoop, yet won't overshadow the flavor of the dip.

Healthy
Snacks & Desserts

Cherry Tomato Hummus Wraps

Amber Sutton
Naches, WA

I love those little tomatoes that you can eat like candy straight from the vine! When I added garden-fresh basil and some other salad ingredients I had on hand, I was delightfully surprised with this resulting summer snack. I think you will be too!

4 T. hummus
4 8-inch flour tortillas, warmed
1 c. cherry tomatoes, halved

1/2 c. Kalamata olives, chopped
1/3 c. crumbled feta cheese
6 sprigs fresh basil, snipped

Spread one tablespoon hummus down the center of each tortilla. Divide remaining ingredients evenly over hummus. To wrap up tortillas burrito-style, turn tortillas so that fillings are side-to-side. Fold in left and right sides of each tortilla; fold top and bottom edges over the filling. Makes 4 servings.

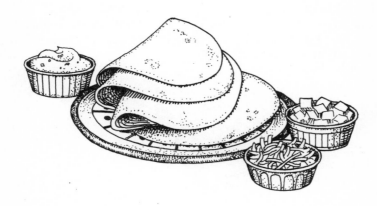

It's a cinch to warm tortillas. Place several tortillas on a microwave-safe plate and cover with a dampened paper towel. Microwave on high for 30 seconds to one minute.

Farmstand Leek Tart

Kelly Alderson
Erie, PA

These tasty morsels look so impressive on a brunch or appetizer tray!
Save time on party days...pre-bake the pastry crust a day ahead,
then add the leek topping shortly before serving.

17.3-oz. pkg. frozen puff
   pastry, divided
2 T. butter
6 leeks, halved lengthwise
   and thinly sliced

salt and pepper to taste

Thaw one sheet of puff pastry according to package directions. Return remaining sheet to the freezer for use in another recipe. On a lightly floured surface, roll out thawed pastry into a 14-by-10-inch rectangle. Cut lengthwise into 2 rectangles; place each on a parchment paper-lined baking sheet. Lightly score rectangles 1/2 inch from the edge with a knife; pierce all over with a fork. Cover and chill for 15 minutes. Bake at 375 degrees for 18 to 20 minutes, until golden. Meanwhile, melt butter in a skillet over medium heat. Add leeks; cover and cook until wilted, about 5 minutes. Uncover; cook until tender, 10 to 12 minutes. Season with salt and pepper. Spoon leek mixture onto crusts; cut into narrow wedges or fingers and serve warm. Makes 8 servings, about 4 pieces each.

Leeks are delicious but can be full of sand when purchased.
Clean them easily by slicing into 2-inch lengths and soaking in
a bowl of cold water. Swish them in the water and drain. Refill
the bowl and swish again until the water is clear. Drain and
pat dry...ready to use.

Healthy
Snacks & Desserts

Creamy Spinach Dip

Karen Augustsson
Frederick, MD

I created this recipe one day for my hungry husband to hold him over until dinner was ready. I've kid-tested this recipe with great success too! Serve with whole-wheat crackers.

10-oz. pkg. frozen chopped
    spinach, cooked
1/4 c. finely shredded Parmesan
    cheese
1/4 c. part-skim ricotta cheese

1/4 c. light sour cream
1/4 c. roasted sunflower
    seed kernels
1/4 t. garlic powder
salt to taste

In a strainer, press spinach to remove as much liquid as possible. Transfer spinach to a bowl. Add remaining ingredients; stir until smooth. If too thick, stir in a little more ricotta cheese to desired consistency. Makes 8 servings, or about 2 cups.

Scoop out the centers of cherry tomatoes, then fill with a dollop of a flavorful, creamy spread. Lighter than crackers and chips...so pretty on an appetizer tray too!

Spicy Broccomole

Michelle Powell
Valley, AL

A delicious, creamy dip or topping for tacos, burritos and quesadillas that's high-protein, low-cal and low-fat. For an extra-spicy flavor, leave in some of the jalapeño seeds.

3 c. fresh or frozen broccoli
    flowerets
1 jalapeño pepper, roasted,
    seeded and chopped
1 green onion, chopped
1/3 c. plain Greek yogurt

3 T. fresh cilantro, chopped
1 t. olive oil
1/4 t. chili powder
1/4 t. garlic powder
1/4 t. salt
1/4 t. pepper

In a saucepan over medium-high heat, cook broccoli in salted water until very soft. Drain well, squeezing out water with a paper towel. Transfer broccoli to a food processor or blender; add remaining ingredients. Process until smooth. If a smoother texture is desired, add a little more olive oil. Serve warm. Makes 10 servings, or about 3 cups.

Dip to go! Spoon some creamy vegetable dip into a
tall plastic cup and add crunchy celery and carrot sticks,
red pepper strips, cucumber slices and snow pea pods. Add a lid
and the snack is ready to tote along. Be sure to keep it chilled.

Healthy
Snacks & Desserts

Fort Worth Bean Dip

Betty Lou Wright
Hendersonville, TN

When our son moved to Texas, we were introduced to some mighty fine Tex-Mex cooking. I make this tasty dip when he comes home, just so he won't miss all the good eatin' in Fort Worth. Use low-fat products if you like. Serve with nacho tortilla chips...delicious!

15-oz. can refried beans
1 bunch green onions, chopped
1-1/2 c. sour cream
1/2 c. cream cheese, softened

1-1/4 oz. pkg. taco seasoning
   mix, or to taste
1 c. shredded Cheddar cheese

Combine all ingredients except cheese in a lightly greased 2-quart casserole dish. Sprinkle cheese on top. Bake, uncovered, at 300 degrees for 45 minutes, or until hot and bubbly. Makes 12 servings, or about 3 cups.

Serve your favorite dip with a twist! Just spread dip onto flour tortillas, roll up jelly-roll style and cut into one-inch slices. Try using colorful flavored wraps like sun-dried tomato & basil, garlic-herb or chipotle chile...top each with a slice of olive or jalapeño pepper.

Cheesy Spinach-Stuffed Mushrooms

Cinde Shields
Issaquah, WA

These warm, savory bite-size beauties always seem to find their way onto my holiday appetizer menu. In fact, I love these mushrooms so much that I even serve them to my family for dinner year 'round with a side of quinoa and a hearty salad.

10-oz. pkg. frozen chopped
    spinach, thawed and
    squeezed dry
1/4 c. cream cheese, softened
1 c. crumbled feta cheese

3/4 t. garlic powder
1/4 t. pepper
24 mushrooms, stems removed
1 c. grated Parmesan cheese

In a bowl, combine all ingredients except mushroom caps and Parmesan cheese; mix well. Spoon mixture into mushrooms; place on a rimmed baking sheet. Sprinkle mushrooms with Parmesan cheese. Bake at 350 degrees for 15 to 20 minutes, until bubbly and heated through. Serve warm. Makes about 8 servings.

Super-simple cheese snacks! Cut several 8-ounce packages of cream cheese into 10 cubes each. Shape cubes into balls and roll in finely chopped pecans, paprika or snipped fresh parsley. Arrange on a plate, cover and pop in the fridge until party time.

Healthy
Snacks & Desserts

Witchy's Chickpea Wraps

Anne Tassé
Orillia, Ontario

I added my own little bit of magic to a simple hummus-type spread and wrapped it in tortillas! These roll-ups are so easy to make, and you can add your own little touches. They're one of the first things to go at all of my gatherings.

19-oz. can garbanzo beans,
  drained and rinsed
1/2 c. fresh parsley or
  dill, chopped
2 to 4 cloves garlic, minced

juice of 1 lemon
1/2 c. olive oil
5 to 6 10-inch flour tortillas,
  any flavor
Optional: lemon wedges

Combine all ingredients except tortillas and lemon wedges in a food processor or blender. Process to a smooth paste, adding a little more olive oil if needed. On each tortilla, spread about 2 tablespoons of mixture out to the edge. Roll up tightly; place tortillas seam-side down on an ungreased baking sheet. Bake at 350 degrees for about 15 to 20 minutes, until edges are lightly crisp. Slice each tortilla into one-inch pieces. Serve with lemon wedges, if desired. Makes 8 servings of 3 pieces each, or 2 dozen.

Need a quick after-school snack to tide the kids over until dinnertime? Just toss together bite-size cereal squares, raisins and a few chocolate-covered candies.

Garden-Fresh Veggie Spread

Lisa Cunningham
Boothbay, ME

This is a quick recipe I created when I had tons of roma tomatoes and zucchini from my garden. By all means, use fresh onions and herbs if you have them. I serve this as a dip with crackers and celery sticks. It's a scrumptious filling for tortilla roll-ups too, just add a little less sour cream.

10 roma tomatoes, diced
1 zucchini, peeled and diced
1/2 c. sweet onion, minced
1 T. fresh parsley, chopped

8-oz. pkg. cream cheese, softened
2 T. Italian salad dressing mix
1 c. sour cream

In a bowl, combine vegetables and parsley; set aside. In a separate bowl, blend cream cheese and dressing mix; add sour cream to desired consistency. Add cream cheese mixture to vegetable mixture; stir well. For best flavor, cover and chill at least 8 hours. Makes 10 servings, or about 5 cups.

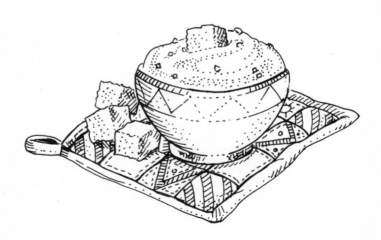

Keep your favorite creamy dip chilled...simply nestle the serving bowl into a larger bowl filled with crushed ice.

Healthy
Snacks & Desserts

Lemony-Fresh Dill Dip

Lisa Blumberg
Knoxville, TN

Enjoy this refreshing dip like we do...by dunking blanched fresh green beans in it. Yummy!

1 c. plain low-fat yogurt
1/3 c. fresh dill, chopped
1 t. lemon zest

1 T. lemon juice
salt and pepper to taste

Combine all ingredients in a bowl; stir well. Cover and chill before serving. Makes 4 servings, or 1-1/3 cups.

The best kind of friend is the kind you can sit on a porch swing with, never say a word, then walk away feeling like it was the best conversation you've ever had.
— Arnold Glasow

Sweet Fruit Salsa

Aimee Shugarman
Liberty Township, OH

My sister-in-law first introduced me to this flavorful salsa on a family camping trip. It has now become our must-have snack whenever we camp together! Serve with cinnamon pita chips.

1 pt. strawberries, hulled and finely diced
1 green apple, cored and finely diced
1 mango, peeled, cored and finely diced

2 T. orange marmalade
1 t. ground ginger
1 t. dried mint

Combine all ingredients in a serving bowl; mix gently. Cover and keep chilled up to 3 days. Makes 8 servings, or about 4 cups.

New plastic sand pails make whimsical party servers for chips and snacks. They're inexpensive, come in lots of bright colors and, perhaps best of all, stack easily so storage is a snap.

Healthy
Snacks & Desserts

Honey Fruit Dip

Nancy Wise
Little Rock, AR

Serve with slices of fresh fruit for delicious dipping.

1-1/3 c. plain Greek yogurt
2 t. honey
1/4 t. orange zest

1 T. orange juice
1/8 t. vanilla extract

Stir together all ingredients in a serving bowl. Cover and chill. Makes 6 servings, or about 1-1/3 cups.

Cinnamon-Sugar Tofu Chips

Elizabeth Wong
Woodinville, WA

*We like to make these fun and crunchy chips for our kids.
If you're not a fan of sweets, toss the chips with smoked
paprika or salt instead.*

2 T. sugar
1 T. cinnamon

1 lb. firm tofu
2 to 3 T. canola oil, divided

Mix cinnamon and sugar in a small bowl; set aside. Carefully cut tofu into thin, chip-size slices or triangles. Heat 2 tablespoons oil in a saucepan over medium heat. Working in small batches, add tofu chips. Make sure each chip gets oil on both sides to ensure it will get crisp, adding more oil for each batch. Cook about 2 minutes, until lightly golden around the edges; flip and cook on other side until crisp. Immediately toss chips in cinnamon-sugar mixture and serve. Makes 4 servings.

Keep bags of sweetened dried cranberries and chopped walnuts
tucked in the cupboard for healthy between-meal snacking.

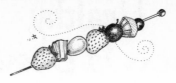

Raspberry Lemonade

Jennifer Niemi
Meadowvale, Nova Scotia

Such a beautiful ruby-red color...when this beverage is served over ice, it just sparkles!

6-inch cinnamon stick, broken
7 c. water, divided
16-oz. pkg. frozen raspberries
   in syrup, thawed

1 c. lemon juice
1/2 c. sugar

Combine cinnamon stick and one cup water in a small saucepan. Bring to a boil over medium-high heat; reduce heat. Cover and simmer for 10 to 15 minutes. Discard cinnamon stick and set aside water to cool. Place a colander over a bowl and strain raspberries well, reserving the syrup; discard berry pulp and seeds. In a a large pitcher, combine cinnamon-flavored water, one cup reserved raspberry syrup, lemon juice and remaining water. Add sugar, stirring to dissolve. Cover and chill; serve over ice. Makes 8 servings.

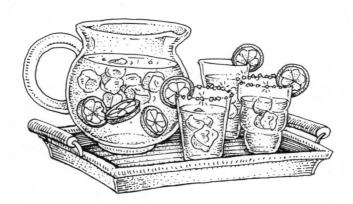

Serve up icy lemonade in frosted-rim glasses! Chill tumblers in the fridge. At serving time, moisten rims with lemon juice or water and dip into a dish of sparkling sugar.

Healthy
Snacks & Desserts

Fabulous Fruit Tea

Becca Jones
Jackson, TN

This fruit tea is so refreshing...it's the best fruit tea I have ever tasted or served! Garnish with an orange slice on the rim of each glass for added appeal.

12 c. water, divided
1 c. sugar
9 tea bags
12-oz. can frozen lemonade
   concentrate, thawed

12-oz. can frozen orange juice
   concentrate, thawed
3 c. pineapple juice

Bring 4 cups water to a boil in a saucepan over high heat. Stir in sugar until dissolved. Remove from heat; add tea bags. Let stand for 8 to 10 minutes to steep; discard tea bags. Pour tea mixture into a large pitcher. Stir in juices and remaining water. Cover and chill; serve over ice. Makes 18 servings.

Garnish summer beverages with fruity ice cubes. Cut watermelon, cantaloupe or honeydew melon into cubes and freeze the cubes on a baking sheet.

Can't-Be-Beet Cake

Janis Parr
Campbellford, Onario

No one would guess this moist and delicious cake is actually good for you. Even the kids love it! For an extra special touch, sometimes I'll garnish the cake with small clusters of seedless green grapes.

3 eggs, separated	1 t. salt
1 c. corn oil	1 t. cinnamon
1-1/2 c. sugar	1 t. vanilla extract
3 T. hot water	1 c. chopped pecans
2 c. all-purpose flour	1 c. beets, peeled and grated
2-1/2 t. baking powder	1 c. carrots, peeled and grated

In a deep bowl, beat egg whites with an electric mixer on high speed until stiff peaks form; set aside. In a separate large bowl, combine egg yolks and remaining ingredients. Mix well; fold in egg whites. Pour batter into a greased and floured 12"x8" baking pan. Bake at 350 degrees for 35 minutes, or until a toothpick inserted in the center tests done. Cool before slicing. Makes 8 servings.

Strawberry "flowers" are a sweet garnish on squares of cake. Slice each strawberry in quarters, being careful not to cut through the stem end, and then gently press a cranberry in the center to create a "flower." Oh-so pretty and tasty too!

192

Healthy
Snacks & Desserts

Agave-Sweetened Pumpkin Cheesecake

Gail Ebey
Canal Fulton, OH

For my diabetic father and other family members watching their diets, I decided to create a pumpkin cheesecake that was a little lighter with agave nectar and low-fat cream cheese. Sugar addicts won't know the difference!

1 c. all-purpose flour
1 c. chopped pecans
1/2 c. butter, melted
8-oz. pkg. low-fat cream cheese,
    softened
1/3 c. agave nectar

3/4 c. canned pumpkin
2 eggs
1 t. vanilla extract
1-1/2 t. cinnamon
1 t. pumpkin pie spice

In a bowl, stir together flour, pecans and melted butter to form a dough. Press dough into a 9" pie plate; pierce several times with a fork. Bake at 350 degrees for 10 minutes; cool slightly. Meanwhile, combine remaining ingredients in a blender. Process until smooth; pour into partially baked crust. Bake at 350 degrees for 35 to 40 minutes, until slightly firm. Cool for about 2 hours; slice into wedges. Makes 8 servings.

Cooked and mashed pumpkin, sweet potatoes and butternut squash can be used interchangeably in quick breads, pies and other dishes. Try a different combination and discover a whole new taste!

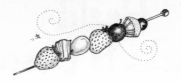

Double-Berry Nut Bars

Linda Nagy
Paris, KY

*Adapted from a favorite family recipe, these easy-to-make
nut bars always get requests for more. The blend of berries
makes these bars colorful as well as tasty.*

2 eggs
1 c. sugar
1 c. all-purpose flour
1/3 c. butter, melted
1/2 c. blueberries, thawed
  if frozen

1/2 c. cranberries, thawed
  if frozen
1/2 c. chopped walnuts
  or pecans
Optional: powdered sugar

In a bowl, with an electric mixer on medium speed, beat eggs until
thick. Gradually beat in sugar until thoroughly blended. Stir in flour
and melted butter; blend well. Add berries and nuts, mixing gently just
until combined. Spread batter evenly in a greased 8"x8" baking pan.
Bake at 350 degrees for 35 to 40 minutes, until golden. Cool; cut into
squares. If desired, dust with powdered sugar. Makes 9 servings.

Garnish cakes, cupcakes or cookies in a jiffy...
sprinkle powdered sugar or cocoa through a doily.

Healthy Snacks & Desserts

No-Bake Yummy Balls

Leona Krivda
Belle Vernon, PA

A fun toss-together yummy snack that's packed with healthy stuff. The grandkids really like them, and my hubby & I love them with a cup of coffee.

1-1/2 c. sweetened flaked
   coconut, toasted and divided
1 c. quick-cooking oats,
   uncooked
1/2 c. creamy peanut butter
1/3 c. honey
1/4 c. ground flax seed

1/4 c. wheat germ
1/4 c. mini semi-sweet chocolate
   chips
1/4 c. chopped walnuts
2 T. dried cranberries or
   cherries, chopped
1 t. vanilla extract

Combine 2/3 cup coconut and remaining ingredients in a bowl. Mix well with your hands. If mixture is too dry, a little more honey or peanut butter may be added. Roll into one-inch balls, then roll in remaining coconut. Place in an airtight container; cover and keep chilled. Makes about 2 dozen balls.

Make a good thing even better...sprinkle with toasted coconut.
Spread sweetened flaked coconut in a shallow pan and bake
at 350 degrees for 7 to 12 minutes, stirring frequently,
until toasted and golden.

Brown Sugar Pineapple Crisp

Arlene Smulski
Lyons, IL

Fresh pineapple is my very favorite fruit! This baked crisp combines a tantalizing taste of paradise, while fresh ginger balances out the sweetness. Top with whipped cream or pineapple sorbet...yum!

1 pineapple, peeled, cored
   and cubed
1/2 c. brown sugar, packed
1/2 c. all-purpose flour
1/4 c. long-cooking oats,
   uncooked
1/8 t. nutmeg

1/2 t. salt
1/4 c. butter, diced
1 T. lime juice
1 T. fresh ginger, peeled
   and grated
1 T. cornstarch
1/3 c. sweetened flaked coconut

Place pineapple in a bowl; set aside. In a separate bowl, combine brown sugar, flour, oats, nutmeg and salt. With your fingers, rub in butter until coarse crumbs form and mixture holds together when squeezed. Cover and chill while making filling. In a small bowl, whisk together lime juice and ginger; stir into pineapple. Sprinkle cornstarch over pineapple; stir again. Transfer pineapple mixture to a lightly greased 9"x9" glass baking pan. Sprinkle crumb mixture and coconut evenly over top. Cover with aluminum foil. Bake at 375 degrees for 20 minutes. Uncover; bake about 10 minutes more, until bubbly around the edges and top is crisp and golden. Cool 10 to 15 minutes before serving. Makes 8 servings.

Offer mini portions of rich cobblers, cakes or pies. Guests can take "just a taste" of something sweet after a big dinner or sample several yummy treats.

Healthy
Snacks & Desserts

"Free" Coconut Cookies

Debbie Blundi
Kunkletown, PA

I call these my "free" cookies because they are sugar-free, fat-free, dairy-free and gluten-free. Whenever I bring them for a church function they are the first to go! Add a teaspoon or two of chopped pecans and carob chips to the dough, if you like.

8 pitted dates
1 very ripe banana, sliced
1-1/2 c. unsweetened flaked
   coconut

1/8 t. vanilla extract
1/8 t. pumpkin pie spice

Place dates in a small bowl; add enough water to cover. Let stand for 2 to 4 hours; drain. Place dates, banana, coconut, vanilla and spice in a food processor or blender. Process until smooth and mixture resembles cookie dough. If mixture is too dry, add a drop or two of water; if too sticky, add a little more coconut. Scoop dough by teaspoonfuls onto ungreased baking sheets, one inch apart. Bake at 325 degrees for 10 to 15 minutes, until tips of coconut start to brown on the bottom; cookies will not brown on top. Let cookies stand on baking sheet until cool; remove to a plate. Leave uncovered for the first day, so cookies don't get too moist. Makes about 16 cookies.

Fun-filled snacks for kids big or little. Fill waffle cones with sliced fresh fruit, then drizzle fruit with puréed strawberries. Yum!

Whole-Wheat Banana Snack Cake

Victoria Mitchel
Gettysburg, PA

You'll be surprised how a recipe with just a few ingredients can come together so quickly, yet taste so good. Perfect with a good friend, conversation and a cup of coffee. My kids love it too...it's their favorite breakfast cake! This recipe contains no eggs.

1-2/3 c. whole-wheat flour
1 c. brown sugar, packed
1 t. baking soda
1 c. ripe banana, mashed

1/3 c. corn or canola oil
1/2 c. water
1/2 t. vanilla extract
Optional: powdered sugar

In a large bowl, combine flour, brown sugar and baking soda; mix and set aside. In a separate bowl, blend remaining ingredients except powdered sugar. Add banana mixture to flour mixture; stir just until moistened. Spoon batter into a greased 9"x9" baking pan. Bake at 350 degrees for 20 to 25 minutes, until center tests done with a toothpick. Cut into squares. Serve warm or cooled, with a dusting of powdered sugar, if desired. Makes 10 servings.

Serve hot spiced coffee with sweet treats. Simply add
3/4 teaspoon pumpkin pie spice to 1/2 cup ground coffee
and brew as usual.

Healthy Snacks & Desserts

No-Bake Granola Bars

Patrice Lindsey
Lockport, IL

Try other dried fruit like blueberries or raisins too!

1/4 c. coconut oil, divided
1 c. creamy peanut butter
1/2 c. honey
2 c. long-cooking oats,
  uncooked

2 c. crispy rice cereal
1 c. sweetened flaked coconut
1/2 c. dried cranberries, chopped
1/2 c. mini semi-sweet chocolate
  chips

Lightly grease a 13"x9" baking pan with a small amount of coconut oil; set aside. In a large saucepan, combine remaining coconut oil, peanut butter and honey. Cook and stir over low heat just until blended and smooth. Remove from heat; add oats, cereal, coconut and cranberries. Stir just until evenly coated and well combined. Let cool about 10 minutes; stir in chocolate chips. Quickly transfer mixture to baking pan; spread evenly with a spatula. Cover with plastic wrap or wax paper; press mixture down evenly and firmly. Refrigerate for one hour before cutting into bars. May be kept tightly covered and refrigerated for up to 10 days. Makes 16 bars.

Keep your family's favorite crunchy snacks handy in big
unbreakable plastic jars, and label each jar with a family face.
Colorful photos glued on each jar will remind snackers
of what's inside.

Strawberry-Lime Yogurt Cake

Cindy Jamieson
Barrie, Ontario

Tart, moist yogurt cakes have always been a favorite of mine. When I decided to make a version using some fresh berries that I had picked with the kids, we all went crazy for it! It's been a most-requested dessert ever since.

2-1/2 c. all-purpose flour,
    divided
1/2 t. baking soda
1/2 t. salt
2 t. lime zest, divided
1 c. butter, softened
1-1/2 c. sugar

3 eggs
3 T. lime juice, divided
1 c. vanilla yogurt
1-1/2 c. strawberries, hulled
    and diced
1 c. powdered sugar

In a bowl, whisk together 2-1/4 cups flour, baking soda and salt. Mix in one teaspoon lime zest; set aside. In a separate large bowl, blend together butter and sugar until light and fluffy. Beat in eggs, one at a time; stir in one tablespoon lime juice. Add flour mixture and yogurt alternately to butter mixture, stirring just until blended. In a separate bowl, toss together strawberries and remaining flour. Gently mix berries into batter. Pour batter into a greased and floured 10" Bundt® pan. Bake at 325 degrees for 60 minutes, or until a toothpick inserted near center of cake tests clean. Cool cake in the pan for 10 minutes; turn out onto a wire rack and cool completely. Whisk together powdered sugar with remaining lime zest and juice; drizzle over top of cake. Makes 12 servings.

There is nothing wrong with the world that a
sensible woman could not settle in an afternoon.

–Jean Giraudoux

Healthy
Snacks & Desserts

Healthy Oatmeal Apple Crisp

Amy Snyder
White Oak, WV

This quick recipe almost tastes too good to believe that it's good for you! You can also add raisins, walnuts or pecans to suit your preference. Top with a scoop of ice cream...yum!

6 c. tart apples, cored and sliced
1/4 c. frozen apple juice
   concentrate, thawed
1 t. cinnamon, divided
1/4 c. butter, softened

3/4 c. quick-cooking oats,
   uncooked
1/4 c. whole-wheat flour
1/3 c. brown sugar, packed

In a bowl, combine apples, apple juice concentrate and 1/2 teaspoon cinnamon. Stir until well mixed. Spread in an 8"x8" glass baking pan sprayed with non-stick vegetable spray. In the same bowl, mix remaining cinnamon and other ingredients until crumbly; sprinkle over apples. Bake, uncovered, at 375 degrees for 25 to 35 minutes, until apples are tender and topping is golden. Serve warm. Makes 8 servings.

Share laughs at family movie night...bring out the home movies from when Mom & Dad were kids. Or share feature films that were extra-special to you when you were growing up.
Pass the popcorn, please!

Refrigerator Pumpkin Bran Muffins

Julie Fehr
Martensville, Saskatchewan

Our four sons love these...they're my family's absolute favorite muffins. Every fall I buy 20 to 30 pie pumpkins to cook and freeze so I'll always have pumpkin purée on hand to make these muffins, but canned pumpkin works well too.

2 c. bran flake cereal
2 c. buttermilk
2 c. cooked pumpkin purée,
   or 15-oz. can pumpkin
1/3 c. butter, melted and slightly
   cooled
2 eggs, beaten
1-1/2 c. all-purpose flour

1 c. whole-wheat flour
1-1/2 c. sugar
2 t. baking powder
1 t. baking soda
1 t. cinnamon
1/2 t. ginger
1/4 t. ground cloves
Optional: 3 T. ground flax seed

Combine cereal and buttermilk in a large bowl; let stand 5 minutes. Add pumpkin, butter and eggs; mix well. In a separate large bowl, mix together flours, sugar, baking powder, baking soda and spices. Add pumpkin mixture to flour mixture; stir until completely moistened. Batter may be baked immediately, or stored up to one week in a tightly covered container in the refrigerator. To bake, spoon batter into lightly greased or paper-lined muffin cups, filling 3/4 full. Bake at 400 degrees for 18 to 20 minutes, until muffin tops are firm to the touch. Makes 2-1/2 dozen.

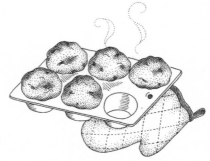

A baker's secret! Grease muffin cups on the bottoms
and just halfway up the sides...the muffins will bake up
nicely puffed on top.

Healthy
Snacks & Desserts

Cranberry-Carrot Loaf

Diane Widmer
Blue Island, IL

My grandmother gave me this recipe. I've updated it by reducing the sugar, replacing the oil with applesauce and adding cranberries. I think you'll agree it's still packed with old-fashioned goodness!

2 c. all-purpose flour
3/4 c. sugar
1-1/2 t. baking powder
1-1/2 t. baking soda
1/4 t. salt
1/2 t. cinnamon
1/2 c. carrot, peeled and
    shredded

1/3 c. low-fat sour cream
1/4 c. unsweetened applesauce
1/4 c. water
2 eggs, lightly beaten
1 c. frozen cranberries

Grease the bottom of a 9"x5" loaf pan; set aside. In a large bowl, mix together flour, sugar, baking powder, baking soda, salt and cinnamon. Stir in carrot to coat. Make a well in center of flour mixture; add sour cream, applesauce, water and eggs. Stir until combined. Slowly stir in cranberries. Spoon batter into pan. Bake on center oven rack at 350 degrees for 60 minutes, or until a toothpick inserted in the center comes out clean. Cool loaf in pan for 15 minutes. Remove to a rack and cool completely. Makes one loaf, about 8 servings.

Warm homemade quick breads are wonderful with creamery butter! For the freshest-tasting butter, keep just one stick in the fridge at a time, and tuck the rest of the package into the freezer.

Freezy Fruit Pops

Stacie Avner
Delaware, OH

Both kids and adults will love these freezer pops made with fresh fruit. Invent new flavors using other favorite soft fruits!

1/2 c. sugar
2 c. boiling water
20-oz. can crushed pineapple
10-oz. pkg. frozen strawberries,
    thawed

6-oz. can frozen orange juice
    concentrate, thawed
5 ripe bananas, mashed
24 3-oz. paper cups
24 wooden craft sticks

In a bowl, dissolve sugar in boiling water. Stir in pineapple with juice and remaining ingredients. In 2 batches, pour mixture into a blender; process until smooth. Ladle into paper cups; set in a pan. Freeze until partially frozen; insert a stick in each cup. Return to freezer until frozen. To serve, peel away cup. Makes 2 dozen pops.

Peachy Fruit Sorbet

Zoe Bennett
Columbia, SC

So refreshing! Garnish with fruit slices.

1 peach, peeled, pitted
    and cubed
1 c. mango, peeled, pitted
    and cubed

1 ripe banana, peeled
    and mashed
2 T. water
1 T. lemon juice

Place fruit on a wax paper-lined baking sheet. Cover and freeze for about 2 hours, until completely frozen. Combine fruit, water and lemon juice in a food processor; process until smooth. Serve immediately, or spoon into a covered container and freeze up to 2 weeks. Makes 4 servings.

Healthy
Snacks & Desserts

Coconut Whipped Cream

Shari Boshart
Durham, NC

Some of my family can't have dairy products, so we created this fabulous topping. We love it dolloped on everything from pumpkin pie to chocolate cake to fresh fruit!

14-oz. can coconut milk
  (not non-fat)

1 T. honey
1 t. vanilla extract

Refrigerate unopened can of coconut milk at least 24 hours. When chilled, the thicker cream will separate and rise to the top. Open can and scoop off the cream; reserve the liquid milk for use in a different recipe. In a deep bowl, beat coconut cream, honey and vanilla with an electric mixer on high speed for 5 to 10 minutes, until fluffy. Serve immediately, or cover and chill for several hours. Makes 4 to 6 servings.

Don't confuse coconut milk with cream of coconut. The labels on the cans may be similar, but coconut milk is thin and smooth, while cream of coconut is thick and sweet.

Watermelon Freezer Pops

Devin Steelman
Perkins, OK

When I was in elementary school, our cafeteria used to sell frozen fresh fruit pops. Watermelon was my favorite flavor! The best part was, the seeds were left in so it was really like eating watermelon ripe from the vine. I would eat as little lunch as possible to save room for as many watermelon pops as time allowed. I've now figured out how to make my own. It's pretty simple!

1 medium watermelon, peeled
    and cubed
1 c. sugar, or to taste

12 to 14 5-oz. foam cups
12 to 14 wooden craft sticks

Place watermelon in a large bowl. Mash with a potato masher, leaving some large chunks unmashed. Stir in sugar; let stand for 10 minutes. Stir and mash again. Ladle into cups, distributing juice evenly. Cover with aluminum foil; insert a stick into each cup. Freeze overnight. Makes 12 to 14 pops.

Watermelon in Balsamic Vinegar

Sonya Labbe
West Hollywood, CA

I tried a dessert similar to this while visiting Italy. Each time it's hot outside and I have company visiting, I like to prepare this unusual and refreshing light dessert or afternoon snack.

4 c. watermelon, cubed, seeds
    removed and chilled
1 to 2 t. sugar

1/4 c. balsamic vinegar
1 t. pepper

Divide watermelon cubes among 4 dessert dishes. In a cup, stir sugar into vinegar until dissolved. Drizzle vinegar mixture over each serving; sprinkle with pepper. Makes 4 servings.

Healthy
Snacks & Desserts

Blueberries & Honey Ice Pops

Tina Wright
Atlanta, GA

These fruity homemade pops are berry delicious!

1 c. blueberries, thawed if frozen
1/2 c. blueberry juice
1/4 c. honey
juice of 1 lime

Optional: 1/4 t. fresh thyme,
   snipped
4 5-oz. paper cups
4 wooden craft sticks

Combine all ingredients in a food processor or blender; process to desired consistency. Ladle into cups; set in a pan and freeze. After one hour, insert a stick into the center of each. Freeze until completely frozen, 2 hours to overnight. To serve, let stand at room temperature several minutes; peel off cup. Makes 4 pops.

Frozen grapes are a scrumptious, healthy treat that's oh-so easy to make! Rinse seedless grapes and pat dry, then arrange in a single layer in a shallow pan. Freeze at least 2 hours, then store in mini plastic zipping bags for grab & go snacking.

Green Tea Cucumber Pops

Elise Johnson
Raleigh, NC

*My church's congregation plants a garden of fruits & vegetables
every summer, delivering to local families what might be the only
fresh food they have. Many people have asked for different ways to
prepare this beautiful produce. This recipe was my idea...it puts a
smile on everyone's face!*

1/2 c. boiling water
1 green tea bag
1 T. fresh mint, chopped
1/8 t. liquid stevia extract
1/2 English cucumber, peeled
   and diced

3 slices honeydew melon,
   peeled and diced
juice of 1 lime
2 T. agave nectar
4 5-oz. paper cups
4 wooden craft sticks

Combine boiling water, tea bag and mint in a cup; let stand for
10 minutes. Discard tea bag. Sweeten tea with stevia extract to taste;
chill. Tea mixture may be prepared ahead of time. In a food processor
or blender, combine cucumber and melon. Add tea mixture, lime juice
and agave nectar; process until smooth. Divide mixture among cups.
Cover and freeze at least 4 hours, inserting a stick in each after
one hour. Makes 4 servings.

Grilled fruit is a terrific dessert...try spooning blueberries into
pitted peach halves. Sprinkle on a little brown sugar, wrap in
aluminum foil and grill until peaches are tender, about 10 minutes.

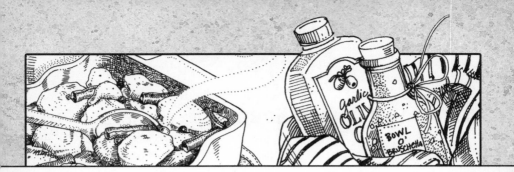

A Homemade

Pantry

Amazing Tomato Sauce

Jen Licon-Conner
Gooseberry Patch

You won't believe the richness real butter adds to this super-simple tomato sauce. Perfect with pasta and grated Parmesan, of course, but we've been known to skip the noodles and make garlic bread to dip in the sauce! Make it with summer's best tomatoes or grab a can from the pantry.

2 c. tomatoes, diced, or 28-oz.
   can tomato purée
1 onion, halved

1/4 c. butter, sliced
2 t. garlic, minced
salt and pepper to taste

In a large saucepan, combine tomatoes with juice, onion halves, butter and garlic. Simmer over medium heat until small bubbles start to form at the edges. Reduce heat to low. Simmer for another 30 minutes, stirring occasionally. Discard onion; add salt and pepper to taste. Cover and refrigerate if not using immediately. Makes about 2-1/2 cups, or 6 servings.

Peel lots of tomatoes in a jiffy! Cut an "X" in the base of each tomato and place them in a deep saucepan. Add boiling water to cover. After 20 to 30 seconds, remove tomatoes with a slotted spoon and drop them into a sinkful of ice water. The peels will slip right off.

A Homemade Pantry

Grandma Gash's Catsup

Melissa Taylor
Saint Peters, MO

My Grandma Gash canned many jars of tomatoes and tomato juice every summer. With spatters of red juice on her old-fashioned flowered apron, she would laugh and we would talk. Grandma passed away in August, 2010, but the memories of her canning will last a lifetime for me. She used this catsup on her famous salmon cakes, hamburgers and fried potatoes...I love it on meatloaf.

2 c. tomatoes, chopped	1/2 t. salt
1 onion, chopped	1/4 t. pepper
1/2 c. sugar	1 T. cornstarch
1/4 c. cider vinegar	2 T. cold water
1 t. celery seed	

Place tomatoes with juice, onion, sugar, vinegar and seasonings in a large heavy saucepan. Bring to a boil over medium heat. Reduce heat to low. Simmer for 20 minutes, stirring occasionally. In a small bowl, dissolve cornstarch in cold water. Add to tomato mixture; cook and stir until thickened. Remove from heat and allow to cool slightly. Ladle into a pint jar; add lid. Keep refrigerated up to 3 weeks. Makes one pint.

Hollowed-out peppers make garden-fresh servers for catsup, relish and mustard! Just cut a thin slice off the bottom so they'll sit flat.

Sweet-and-Sour Sauce

Andrea Heyart
Aubrey, TX

Toss with meat and veggies for a delicious meal or use as a dipping sauce for your favorite snack! I sometimes add diced green peppers and green onions to this sauce for added flavor.

1/3 c. cider vinegar
1/2 c. sugar
1/4 c. brown sugar, packed
1/2 c. pineapple juice

1/3 c. water
1 T. plus 1 t. soy sauce
3 T. catsup
2 T. cornstarch

Combine all ingredients in a saucepan. Bring to a boil over medium heat, stirring frequently. Reduce heat to medium-low. Continue cooking and stirring until thickened. Use immediately, or cover and refrigerate up to one week. Makes about 1-1/2 cups, or 4 servings.

Gingered Stir-Fry Sauce

Judy Taylor
Butler, MO

This recipe can be made ahead and tucked in the fridge, then used when you prepare the rest of your stir-fry ingredients.

2-1/2 c. chicken or beef broth
1/2 c. sherry or apple juice
1/2 c. soy sauce
3 T. red wine vinegar
3 T. brown sugar, packed

1/3 c. cornstarch
2 t. fresh ginger, peeled
   and grated
4 cloves garlic, pressed

Combine all ingredients in a blender. Process until smooth and well blended. May be kept in a covered quart jar in the refrigerator up to 3 weeks. Shake or stir well before using. Makes about 4 cups, or 8 servings.

Look for inexpensive Asian-themed plates, bowls and teacups at an import store. They'll make even the simplest stir-fry meals special.

A Homemade Pantry

Fresh Tartar Sauce

Patricia Madden
Puyallup, WA

This is my mother's recipe. I think you'll agree a freshly made batch of tartar sauce makes any fish meal much tastier!

1 c. mayonnaise-style salad
   dressing
1/2 c. sweet pickle relish

2 T. onion, chopped
1 T. lemon juice

In a bowl, mix together all ingredients. Use immediately, or cover and refrigerate up to one week. Makes about 1-1/2 cups, or 12 servings.

Thousand Island Dressing

Alice Randall
Nacogdoches, TX

I have enjoyed this recipe since 1957, when I found it in the booklet that came with my first electric mixer. It's delicious ladled over crisp lettuce wedges. Recently, when I hosted our pastor and other guests, I thought they might be tired of it so bought a bottled dressing...they wouldn't have it!

1 c. mayonnaise
1/4 c. bottled chili sauce
1-1/2 t. Worcestershire sauce

1 egg, hard-boiled, peeled and
   finely chopped

Place all ingredients in a small bowl. Beat with an electric mixer on medium speed until well blended. Use immediately, or cover and refrigerate up to one week. Makes about 1-1/2 cups, or 6 servings.

Cream Of Chicken Soup

Andrea Heyart
Aubrey, TX

One night I realized I was out of the canned cream soup that my recipe called for. I gave this delicious lower-sodium alternative a try... it's wonderful! You can add sautéed chopped mushrooms, onion or celery to make different kinds of soup.

1/4 c. butter, sliced
1/2 c. all-purpose flour
10-1/2 oz. can low-sodium
  chicken broth
12-oz. can evaporated milk

1/2 t. onion powder
salt and pepper to taste
1/4 to 1/2 c. cooked chicken,
  shredded

Melt butter in a saucepan over medium-low heat. Stir in flour, forming a thick paste. Whisk in broth and milk. Cook over medium heat, stirring occasionally, until mixture thickens. Stir in seasonings and chicken. Use immediately, or cover and refrigerate up to 3 days. Makes the equivalent of two 10-3/4 ounce cans of cream soup.

Handy Cream Soup Mix

Cathy Hillier
Salt Lake City, UT

A terrific little mix to keep tucked in the pantry.

2 c. non-fat powdered milk
3/4 c. cornstarch
1/4 c. chicken or beef bouillon
  granules

2 T. dried, minced onion
1 t. dried thyme
1 t. dried basil
1/2 t. pepper

Mix all ingredients well; divide evenly into 10 plastic zipping bags. To use: In a saucepan, combine 1-1/4 cups cold water, one bag soup mix and one teaspoon butter. Cook and stir until thickened. Makes the equivalent of ten 10-3/4 ounce cans of cream soup.

A Homemade Pantry

Corn Muffin Mix

Melanie Lowe
Dover, DE

I love having this mix on hand for Mexican-style casseroles with a cornbread topping...and just for whipping up a quick batch of corn muffins to go with chili!

2-2/3 c. all-purpose flour
2 c. yellow cornmeal
3/4 c. sugar

1/4 c. baking powder
1 t. salt

Mix together all ingredients; divide evenly into 4 plastic zipping bags. Keep in a cool, dry place or in the freezer. Each bag may be added directly to a recipe calling for one corn muffin mix. To bake muffins, combine one bag muffin mix, 2 tablespoons oil, 1/3 cup milk and one beaten egg. Stir well; fill 6 greased muffin cups 1/2 full. Bake at 400 degrees for 15 to 20 minutes. Makes the equivalent of four 8-1/2 ounce boxes of corn muffin mix.

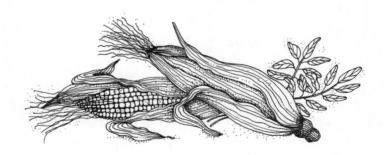

Cornmeal comes in yellow, white and even blue...the choice is yours! Stone-ground cornmeal is more nutritious than regular cornmeal, but has a shorter shelf life. If you're freezing your homemade Corn Muffin Mix, that won't be a problem.

Best-Ever Ranch Dressing

Sara Blankenship
Barton, NY

This is the best ranch dressing I've ever had and it's healthy...
you can't beat that! Serve as a scrumptious salad dressing
or as a yummy dip.

2 c. plain yogurt
1/4 to 1/2 c. mayonnaise
1 t. dried parsley
1/2 t. celery flakes
1/2 t. garlic powder
1/2 t. onion powder

1/4 t. paprika
1/4 t. dill weed
1/2 t. salt
1/4 t. pepper
Optional: 1/8 t. cayenne pepper,
   or to taste

In a bowl, combine all ingredients; mix well. Cover and refrigerate for
several hours to overnight before serving. Keep refrigerated up to
2 weeks. Makes about 2-1/4 cups, or 18 servings.

Onion-Poppy Seed Dressing

Joyceann Dreibelbis
Wooster, OH

This easy salad dressing is delicious on all kinds of salads.
It's sweet, tangy and oniony, and it won't separate. You'll love it!

1/3 c. cider vinegar
1/2 c. sugar
1/2 sweet onion, cut into wedges

1 t. dry mustard
1 c. canola oil
1 t. poppy seed

In a blender, combine vinegar, sugar, onion and mustard. Cover and
process until blended and smooth. While processing, gradually add oil
in a steady stream. Stir in poppy seed. Cover; keep refrigerated up to
one week. Makes about 2 cups, or 16 servings.

A Homemade Pantry

Basic Balsamic Dressing

Kelly Ritter
Freeville, NY

*Everyone always asks me, "What brand of dressing is this?"
never suspecting it's homemade. I use this dressing for tossed salad,
pasta salad and sometimes we even marinate chicken in it!*

2/3 c. extra-virgin olive oil
1/2 c. balsamic vinegar
2 cloves garlic, minced
2 T. dried parsley

2 t. dried basil
2 t. dried, minced onion
1 t. salt

Mix together all ingredients in an airtight dressing container. Cover
and shake well; let stand for 2 hours before serving. Store at room
temperature up to 4 weeks. Makes about 1-1/2 cups, or 11 servings.

Oo-la-la French Dressing

Ann Brandau
Cheboygan, MI

*My mom always kept this salad dressing on hand. It's the best
red French dressing I have tasted...so good!*

1/2 c. sugar
1/2 c. brown sugar, packed
1/2 c. corn or canola oil
1/3 c. catsup
1/4 c. cider vinegar

2 to 3 T. lemon juice
1 t. paprika
1 t. salt
Optional: 1/2 c. onion, grated

Place all ingredients in a blender and blend well. Pour into a jar; cover
and refrigerate up to 4 weeks. Makes about 2 cups, or 16 servings.

Stash bags of fresh salad greens in the fridge along with
chopped veggies and even crispy bacon left from breakfast.
Toss with dressing for a salad ready in a flash!

Index

Index

Index